D1314836

SCHOOLING IN A PLURAL CANADA

Multilingual Matters

**Please contact us for the latest book information:
Multilingual Matters, Bank House, 8a Hill Road,
Clevedon, Avon BS21 7HH, England.**

MULTILINGUAL MATTERS 23
Series Editor: Derrick Sharp

Schooling in a Plural Canada

John R. Mallea

MULTILINGUAL MATTERS LTD
Clevedon · Philadelphia

For Paula

Library of Congress Cataloging in Publication Data

Mallea, John R.
   Schooling in a plural Canada/John R. Mallea.
      p. cm. — (Multilingual matters; 23)
   Bibliography: p.
   Includes index.
   1. Educational sociology—Canada—Case studies. 2. Pluralism
(Social sciences)—Canada—Case studies. 3. Educational
anthropology—Canada—Case studies. I. Title. II. Series.
III. Series: Multilingual matters (Series); 23.
LC191.8.C2M35   1989
370.19′ 0971—dc19   88-25857

British Library Cataloguing in Publication Data

Mallea, John R. (John Richard), *1936–*
   Schooling in a plural Canada
   (Multilingual matters; 23).
   1. Canada. Education. Effects of pluralism
   I. Title
   370′ . 971

     ISBN 1-85359-030-4
     ISBN 1-85359-029-0   Pbk

Multilingual Matters Ltd
Bank House, 8a Hill Road   &   242 Cherry Street
Clevedon, Avon BS21 7HH   Philadelphia, Pa 19106–1906
England   U.S.A.

Typeset by Editorial Enterprises, Torquay, Devon
Printed and bound in Great Britain by Short Run Press, Exeter

Contents

Preface

This text adopts a case-study approach to the analysis of schooling in a plural society. It is divided into two parts. The first part provides a critical review of relevant theory; the second focuses on the application of this theory in the Canadian context. A summary and conclusions chapter underlines the importance of employing alternative theoretical concepts and frameworks.

Part I begins by setting out the limits of traditional theories of pluralism, race and ethnic relations, and schooling. This is followed by a discussion of contemporary forms of pluralism. In addition to cultural pluralism: normative, institutional, structural, political and socio-economic forms of pluralism are discussed. These are then juxtaposed with theories and concepts drawn from the new sociology of education literature. Reproduction, correspondence and resistance theories of schooling are reviewed and their potential contribution to our understanding of schooling in plural societies analyzed. Particular attention is paid to the relevance of concepts such as cultural hegemony, cultural capital and cultural legitimation.

In Part II, following a brief historical review of the conflictual nature of schooling in Canada, three competing views of Canadian culture and society (monocultural, bicultural and multicultural) are described and their contradictions and tensions discussed. Educational systems, it is argued, are part of a much broader framework of interlocking economic, political and cultural systems. Within these systems, schools frequently serve as arenas in which existing public policies are frequently contested and resisted. Three contemporary Canadian examples of conflict over culture and schooling are examined: aboriginal self-government; official language minority educational rights; and heritage language instruction.

A 'Summary and Conclusions' chapter brings the text to a close.

Acknowledgements

The initial motivation for developing this text grew out of a desire to assist students seeking conceptual and theoretical frameworks within which to study schooling in a plural Canada. The task has been a challenging one and is obviously far from complete. Yet, while much work remains to be done, it is hoped that the review of relevant theory contained in the following pages will help provide them with a starting point for their studies.

I wish to thank the staff of the Multiculturalism Directorate, Secretary of State for funding this project and colleagues and graduate students at the Ontario Institute of Studies for providing a supportive environment in which to write. My thanks, too, to Paula de Coito, Yoko Ueda, Marion Morgan, Gillian Pattison, Andrea Playter, Glen Harasymchuk, Russell Medvedev and David Wilkie. Their assistance, and that of others who have helped along the way, is greatly appreciated. As is usual in these matters, responsibility for errors of style or substance is mine alone.

John R. Mallea
Brandon, 1988

Introduction

A renewed exploration of the realities and dilemmas of contemporary pluralism, in modern and developing countries, capitalist and socialist economies alike, has been taking place over the past several decades. International bodies, governments, private foundations and scholars representing an array of disciplines have all been engaged in this exploration. The result has been an impressive growth in the literature on the place and function of ethnicity in the modern world.

Efforts to explain the origins and significance of this interest have failed to reach consensus, yet agreement on one central overriding fact has emerged — that racial and ethnic issues continue to pose important questions for mankind as we approach the twenty-first century. Among the broad, general issues which give rise to a renewed interest in ethnicity and pluralism as they affect our changing world are the break-up of Western colonial societies, the pluralistic make-up of an increasing number of societies (including newly-independent ones), the homogenizing effects of mass culture, and the alienation of groups stemming from loss of individual privacy, bureaucratization and the externalization of personal relations. The underlying values and assumptions of the post-industrial state are being challenged and the perceived material advantages of urban, secular cultures are being weighed against the concomitant loss of identity and belonging and are being found wanting. In addition, the growing recognition of the interdependent nature of the world's economies has prompted speculation on the nature of the modern nation-state.

Revised forms and interpretations of traditional nationalism are being advanced, especially in culturally diverse nations in which state policy has dictated a resolutely monocultural, monolingual format. Paradoxically, these developments are taking place in democratic states which have emphasized the values of cultural orthodoxy and assimilation (albeit often couched in humanitarian terms). Here coercive political power has been employed to enforce the cultural hegemony of the dominant group. And the latter's culture has been 'bolstered up by the full authority of a government bureaucracy and propagated by mass media and a compulsory system of education' (Smolicz, 1979: 9).

The role of schooling is indeed central to these developments. For as Joshua Fishman has observed:

> the need for identity, for community, to make modernity sufferable, is greater than it was and will become greater yet, and woe to the élites — in universities, governments and industries — who do not recognize this or even worse, who consider it to be only a vestigial remnant of nineteenth-century thinking. (1972: 83).

These needs are not transitory but enduring. Ethno-cultural groups have a vitally important contribution to make in meeting them and a system of schooling which encourages these groups to do so can be of inestimable value.

Such propositions are of course not universally supported. There is the counter-argument that differing sectional values are a profound source of instability in plural societies (Smith, 1965). And, federal societies almost by definition, it seems, experience such tensions (Watts, 1970) and give rise to the following questions: How can the values of individualism and pluralism be pursued simultaneously? Does the existence of racial and cultural diversity necessarily result in reduced levels of social cohesion? Can any society that embraces a monistic view of culture be considered democratic? What form might consensual theories of government take in plural societies? Is conflict between dominant and subordinate groups endemic in plural societies? How much decentralization can federal political systems cope with in responding to the legitimate aspirations of minority cultural groups? To what extent can (or should) communal development be defined in terms of secular, universal and material values? Does the concept of valid community lie in the extent to which it creates and maintains its own distinctive cultural norms? What levels of tolerance for contradiction and ambiguity can and should exist in plural societies? Do contradictions help maintain political systems by containing the seeds of necessary change? And what contribution have the social sciences to make in helping answer these and related questions?

In a curious display of reductionism, many social scientists have until very recently underemphasized the importance of ethnicity in their analyses of modern social systems. Some have falsely assumed that ethnic groups would gradually fade away and that, while the process would need to be cushioned during periods of transition, these groups would ultimately lose their meaning and utility for educated, urbanized and industrialized members of the group. Others have underemphasized the importance of minority group cultures by choosing to endow with a higher intrinsic value the cultural norms of dominant groups. Still others have, for reasons best known to themselves, emphasized class to the virtual exclusion of race and ethnicity. Indeed, in 1970 Schermerhorn was able to comment thirty years after the fact that Louis Wirth's 'brilliant analysis of the diverse aims that arise among subordinate ethnic groups in response to varying circumstances and its implications are still relatively unexplored' (Schermerhorn, 1970: 78).

This criticism applies with particular force in the field of education. Much 'cultural indigestion' has been experienced in an effort to find a *modus vivendi* between proponents of general culture and those supportive of plural cultures (Itzkoff, 1969). Sociologists of education, for example, have given scant attention to the argument that race and ethnicity might possess as much significance as social class in explaining social stratification, stability and conflict (Singleton, 1977). The need to study variations in the provision of education in multiracial, multicultural societies has only slowly and relatively recently been recognized (Watson, 1979). Much of the language employed to analyse race relations in education appears dated and inadequate. Minority perspectives on majority views of what should constitute core culture and curriculum in the schools are few in number and difficult to locate (Willis, 1983). And in Canada analyses of culture and schooling are for the most part largely atheoretical (Mallea, 1987).

This absence of theory has provided the stimulus for the present work. And, because the area is largely uncharted territory, a number of challenges were presented. There is the challenge, for example, of integrating theories drawn from a variety of literatures — sociology, culture, pluralism, schooling, and race and ethnic relations. Much of this theoretical literature deals only marginally with the role of the school. Thus the case-study approach as adopted here is essentially exploratory. It aims at stimulating discussion rather than bringing closure to a highly complex issue. For while much has been written about multicultural education, most analysts agree that it has only rarely been informed by theory. Yet, since the question of schooling in a plural Canada is so controversial, the need for informing theory is all the more evident. And, equally, if theory is to inform educational policy and practice it needs to be applied to concrete situations and settings.

PART I:
Theory

The approach adopted in Part I consists of examining three related bodies of literature and drawing from them relevant theoretical insights. Chapter 1 examines traditional theories of pluralism, race and ethnic relations, and schooling and concludes that no comprehensive theory of schooling in plural societies is currently available.

Chapter 2 reviews the contemporary literature on pluralism and pays special attention to the work of that outstanding theorist of comparative ethnic relations: R. A. Schermerhorn. His efforts to draw on both structural-functionalism and power-conflict theories are addressed as the importance he places on the value of dialectical analysis. The value of the latter form of analysis in examining the nature of schooling in a plural society is discussed along with the application of the concepts of cultural, normative, political, structural and socio-economic pluralism.

Chapter 3 focuses on theoretical insights drawn from the new sociology of education literature. The critique this literature offers of traditional sociological theories of education is examined along with the alternatives it proposes: reproduction theory, correspondence theory and resistance theory. The relation between culture and schooling is also examined by way of a number of linked theoretical concepts: cultural hegemony, cultural reproduction, cultural capital, cultural legitimation and cultural resistance. Each concept is reviewed in turn and its analytical power assessed.

Discussion of these theoretical contributions underlines the fact that public school systems are not as autonomous as earlier sociologists of education would have us believe. On the contrary, they form part of a much larger and interlocking pattern of political, economic, social and cultural structures, institutions, and processes. This pattern, moreover, is shaped by a complex set of power differentials in which dominant groups exercise considerable control over public school systems. These validate the dominant culture, marginalize minority cultures and subsequenty give rise to resistance on the part of minority ethno-cultural groups.

1 The limits of traditional theory

Introduction

The problem of analysing schooling in a plural society like Canada is that the relevant theoretical literature, in addition to being multifaceted and complex, is beset with several important limitations. Pre-eminent among these is the fact that virtually no comprehensive theories of Canadian schooling exist. Another is that prevailing liberal and conservative perspectives of schooling, along with the assumptions that inform them, are rarely the subject of in-depth scrutiny and appraisal. A third limitation is that contemporary macro-theoretical analyses of Canadian education, drawing on the disciplines of political studies and economics, are distinguished in large part by their absence.

A similar situation exists in the Canadian theoretical literature on pluralism, race relations and culture. Theories of pluralism and plural societies normally do not contain in-depth analyses of the role of the school. Where schooling is examined, the inquiry usually proceeds in terms of its relationship to normative and cultural pluralism; political and economic pluralism are rarely addressed. More recently, though, efforts have been made to distinguish between normative pluralism and the realities of school practice.

Where the analysis of schooling is concerned, the theoretical literature on race and ethnic relations also exhibits some of the above limitations. No comprehensive theory of race and ethnic relations in education exists. Classificatory systems and typologies exist, but their explanatory power is necessarily limited. Analyses of race and ethnic relations, moreover, have most frequently been pursued from the perspective of majority or dominant groups. Studies of minority schooling from the perspective of subordinate groups are rare, and the contested nature of race and ethnic relations in education has been underemphasized.

Theories of culture, expecially theories of cultural transmission, are plentiful. In general, however, they place stress on concepts such as stability, cohesion and consensus. Notions of controversy, conflict and innovation are correspondingly downplayed.

The cumulative impact of these limitations is severe. Explicit theoretically based frameworks are infrequently employed, while normative ideological statements abound. There is, then, a conscious need for the identification and development of theoretical concepts and frameworks that will inform our understanding of schooling in a plural Canada. We begin the task of identification by reviewing the contributions of the theoretical literature to date.

Theories of pluralism

That Canada is frequently referred to as a plural society is rarely questioned (Ossenberg, 1971; Bullivant, 1981); what is understood by this reference, however, is less clear.

Notions of pluralism (mainly but not exclusively used in the past by anthropologists) underwent considerable redefinition in the 1960s and came to be applied to the analysis of modern as well as traditional societies (Newman, 1973; Gordon, 1973). In contemporary usage, pluralism can refer to the presence of distinct social and cultural groups *within a single polity*, sharing a common economic system that makes them interdependent, but enabling them to maintain a greater or lesser degree of autonomy (Van den Berghe, 1973, italics added). It is characterized by the presence of groups possessing both historical continuity (Smith, 1965) and relative socio-economic status (Isaacs, 1975). Their position in the hierarchical order is differentiated by one or more of the following characteristics: race, class, or culture.

Redefinition of the concept of pluralism also led to renewed efforts to break it down into its constituent parts. Newman (1973) distinguished between what he termed integrative and segregated pluralism — the former referring to a context in which more than one ethnic group shared the same geographical area, the latter one in which different groups occupied distinct territorial units. Gordon (1973) also wrote of two types of pluralism: liberal and corporate. Liberal pluralism he characterized by the absence, even prohibition, of any racial, religious, linguistic or national-origin group possessing standing before the law or government.

Corporate pluralism involved the recognition of these groups as legally constituted entities, on the basis of which, depending on their size and influence, economic and political rewards were allocated. Elements of these types of pluralism can be found in Canada. They possess, as Young (1979) has pointed out, some value for the analysis of public schooling.

These analytical divisions or categories of pluralism serve to remind us of the dangers of assuming that the cultural aspect of pluralism is the only or even the most important feature of a plural society. Such an assumption thus helped mask the real nature of conflicts between dominant and subordinate groups and blurred the political nature of schooling, the most important feature of a plural society. The existence of these distinct analytical categories also draws our attention to the importance of centripetal and centrifugal tendencies in achieving and maintaining national integration.

> Centripetal tendencies refer both to cultural trends such as acceptance of common values, styles of life, etc, as well as structural features like increased participation in a common set of groups, associations, and institutions. To keep the two aspects analytically distinct, it seems tenable to refer to the first as assimilation, and the second as incorporation . . . Conversely, centrifugal tendencies among sub-ordinate groups are those that foster separation from the dominant group or from societal bonds in one respect or another. Culturally this most frequently means retention and presentation of the group's distinctive tradition in spheres like language, religion, recreation, etc. (Schermerhorn, 1970: 81)

Thus where dominant and subordinate groups share these tendencies, whether centripetal or centrifugal, an agreed-upon form of integration is likely to occur. Where they do not, integrative processes are likely to break down and conflicts result. All plural societies face the challenge of achieving a necessary level of integration: political, economic, social and cultural. What is understood by 'integration', the means by which it is sought, and the degree to which it is achieved, varies greatly from country to country (LaBelle & White, 1980).

However, four types of integration may usefully be discussed in this context: cultural, social, normative and structural. The first, cultural integration, refers to the cohesion of diverse parts of any culture and the inner unity of its socio-cultural systems. The second, social integration, results from bringing together the various elements of a social system to constitute a whole. The third, normative integration, is more ideological or value-oriented and emphasizes the degree of consistency between cultural standards and the conduct of personal lifestyles (*International Encyclopedia of the Social Sciences*, 1968). The fourth, structural integration, can be broken down into three broad sub-processes: primary, secondary, and identificational. Primary structural integration has been described as the degree of participation by individuals in institutions established by and for an ethnic or linguistic group other than their own. Secondary structural integration refers to participation in the major institutions (economic, political, and educational, and so on) of the larger society. Identificational integration is the end result of a process whereby another ethnic collectivity becomes one's primary reference group (Kallen *et al.*, 1982).

Despite these helpful conceptual clarifications, use of the term integration remains problematical. For example, according to Itzkoff (1969), although integrationists stress equality along with the need for unity, the language of their arguments bears a strong resemblance to that of an older assimilationist tradition. And even though people today enjoy a wider range of contacts than ever before, they only feel integrated in terms of their functional role, not in terms of personal belonging. Coercive integrationist policies cannot force changes in private action, successful integration requires mutual acquiescence. No society can exist without a certain amount of common social will (Smith, 1965).

If we are to determine how this common social will might be attained and then maintained in a plural society, we need to understand the basis upon which the present social order rests, and the nature and quality of its race and ethnic relations. Two major theoretical perspectives have been employed in studies of these issues — consensus theory and conflict theory. As its name implies, consensus theory posits that social order is best achieved by consensus mediated by agencies such as the state, political parties, and the school.

Consensus theory adopts the view that societies can only persist if total system needs are satisfied. System maintenance, therefore, is the primary function of public institutions and structures, selective emphasis being placed on characteristics such as conservation, stability and predictability.

Conflict theory, on the other hand, stresses the importance of competition, recognizes the existence of significant power differentials, and advances the view that contest and struggle, not consensus and accommodation, are the key elements in the establishment, maintenance and reproduction of the dominant social order.

These two theoretical traditions have been ably summarized and reviewed by Schermerhorn (1970) who considers integration to be a problem of legitimation, cultural congruence, and reciprocal goal definition, with authority being the core relation, and power differentials being crucial to its resolution. Viewed from this perspective, integration is a dynamic and continuing process rather than a completed state. It is a process in which formations are continually modified and changed. It is relative rather than absolute, situational rather than all-embracing, and corrective rather than self-subsistent. Thus to conceive of integration and conflict in absolute or dichotomous terms, or to seek complete linkages at every point is naive. Contexts exist in which integration can only occur in and through conflict, and there are contexts where conflict is necessary if a new order of integration is to be attained.

No national society can continue to exist for long without a minimal sharing of common values. In other words, a moral as well as a political consensus is required. To achieve this in a plural, as opposed to a more homogeneous, society gives rise to a particular set of complex philosophical and political dilemmas (Watson, 1979) which have long exercised the minds of political philosophers and educators. At the global level, Itzkoff (1969), for example, saw the crucial question as being how to integrate vast numbers of racial, ethnic and linguistic groups into a world community whilst simultaneously retaining their heritage. At the national level, he saw it as a problem of constituent groups deemphasizing old cultural forms, reinforcing those that could make it into the future, and gradually establishing one culturally varied but united political, economic and intellectual community.

The most common approach to resolving the pluralist dilemma, perhaps, is that which attempts to build consensus around universal or core values. The idea of universal values, closely linked to the belief that human beings possess universal qualities, finds its philosophical roots in the Enlightenment ideal of universal humanity. Core values, on the other hand, draw on a more particular, normative ideological tradition. Both sets of values are frequently embedded deep in a culture, taken for granted, and accepted almost without question. Both, however, contain fundamentally contradictory elements.

As Novak (1983) has pointed out, accepting the premise that human beings possess universal qualities does not require acceptance of the ideal of universal humanity. The interior liberty which leads us to value the dignity of each person also teaches as to respect the principle of individual differences. Universal reason, therefore, points us in a direction opposite to that suggested by the principle of universality. A similar situation obtains in the case of core values. Western society's view of the man–nature relationship takes for granted that nature exists merely to serve man (a view, incidentally, that underlines much of modern science and technology). It is a view, however, which is not shared by many aboriginal and non-Western societies.

The concept of universal and core values is in fact considerably more problematic than is usually recognized. In the Anglo-Saxon culture, Smolicz & Secombe (1977) observes, considerable emphasis is placed on individualism, independence and self-reliance at the expense of close group ties. These values, supported by legal as well as social and moral sanctions, have in turn become deeply embedded in the Australian political and economic systems. The dominant group sees them as core values. But Australia, he points out, is a multiracial, multi-ethnic society in which cultural diversity is not only recognized but encouraged. Some cultural groups do not place the same emphasis on individualism and its related virtues; rather, they stress communal or group values. How then, Smolicz asks, are these groups, especially the aboriginal groups, to relate to the dominant or core values? How are they to construct their personal identity systems in the context of this relationship? How are state-supported educational systems to take account of these differences?

The plural dilemma in education is evidenced in the ideas of the educational philosopher, John Dewey, whose works exhibit an underlying ambivalence concerning unity and diversity. His concept of human nature and society led him to ambivalence concerning unity and diversity. It also led him to embrace the idea of a plural society, a society composed of self-regulating communities opening itself up to the larger world and entering into dialogue with others. When he attempted to reconcile this approach with the melting-pot approach to what constituted American society and culture, he confronted very real problems. Similarly, his ideas on social reconstruction failed to resolve the issue of coercion that was subtly and psychologically exerted to conform individuals and groups to this pattern. It was no accident, therefore, that 'the so-called cult of social adjustment in its most extravagant misinterpretations resulted in such blatantly conformist tendencies in the schools'. (Itzkoff, 1969: 18)

That Dewey's dilemma is still very much our dilemma is clearly recognized by Bullivant in *Pluralism: Cultural Maintenance and Evolution* (1981) where he observes that the problem is to accommodate two views of society:

On the one hand, the theory of democratic pluralism is mainly concerned with the issue of reconciling the competition that occurs between pluralist groups in a society with the need to preserve cohesion in the nation-state as a whole. On the other hand, cultural pluralism tries to explain how ethno-cultural and racial groups are able to maintain and gain respect for their heritages and identities, in the face of often hostile pressure from the majority groups to assimilate. (p. 106)

The dilemma is a very real one. Allowing democracy full rein may help provide the educational wants of individuals and groups, but in doing so it risks weakening the cohesiveness of the nation-state. Movement in this direction interferes too much with what he terms the enculturation imperative, the need to pass on enough of a common culture to each succeeding generation (Bullivant, 1981).

At the school and classroom level, teachers are expected to help socialize children in accordance with traditional mainstream values while at the same time preparing them for life in a pluralist society and global community (Lynch & Plunkett, 1973). Yet, how this is to be accomplished is rarely spelled out or made clear.

In summary then, there are at least five reasons why traditional theories of pluralism offer limited aid in helping resolve the dilemmas and contradictions inherent in education in multiracial, multicultural societies. First, the dialectic we have observed between the universal and particular cannot be resolved by appeal to any all-encompassing set of principles; instead it must be worked out generation by generation in the context of the day (Itzkoff, 1969). Second, because plural societies 'are characterized in part by the co-existence of autonomous but non-complementary sub-societies which do not share common values, what coherence exists cannot be fully accounted for by value consensus' (Watson, 1982: 188). Third, theories of pluralism are inadequate as a statement of what constitutes the arena of political contention and decision-making. They lack a theory of power and fail to examine power relations, decision-making, and policy formulation at the local community level in terms of the broader societal structure of power (Halebsky, 1976). Fourth, theories of pluralism frequently ignore the tensions between political democracy and economic inequality (Giroux, 1983a). Fifth, and most particularly, theories of pluralism rarely discuss schooling except in the very limited context of cultural pluralism. As a consequence, they downplay conflicting issues and fail to confront the importance of power differentials and the ordering of power relations in the structuring of state-aided public education.

Theories of race and ethnic relations

Both consensus and conflict theories have been employed in the analysis of race and ethnic relations. Consensus theorists have tended to express their analyses in terms of majority–minority group relations and have frequently restricted their focus to matters linguistic or cultural. Conflict theorists, on the other hand, have generally examined the economic and political dimensions of race and ethnicity in terms of dominant–subordinate group relations. And, while both theoretical approaches have something to offer, the conflict perspective possesses superior explanatory value in understanding the complex relationships that exist between culture and schooling in a plural society.

The concept 'dominant group' refers to that collectivity within a society which has the power to establish and allocate society's major rewards; this collectivity also possesses pre-eminent authority to function as guardian and sustainer of the controlling value system. The dominant group may be a majority ethnic group, a restricted élite, or a temporary or permanent coalition of interest groups (Schermerhorn, 1970). Conversely, a subordinate group possesses less power, privilege and prestige. Racial and ethnic groups, of course, can be either dominant or subordinate. In any given politically defined territorial unit, however, one such group is usually dominant, although in plural societies its exercise of power may vary by region, province or community.

A basic question in all racially and ethnically plural societies is whether the dominant group believes subordinate groups should assimilate or retain their cultural distinctiveness.

> From the standpoint of power-conflict theory one can view each ethnic group as being in an embattled position, fighting for its life, its identity, or its prestige, subject to perpetual constraints that threaten its survival, its freedom, or its life chances in a precarious world. (Schermerhorn, 1970)

Power, in this context, is exercised rather than possessed (Giroux, 1981), and is an attribute of existing political and economic relations (Apple, 1979). To a considerable extent, these relations are responsible for selecting and shaping a society's core culture. Thus the racial or ethnic group with control over the power structure of the state usually attempts to monopolize most of its socializing and enculturating functions. It asserts a form of 'dominant monism' (Singleton, 1977) and traditionally enlists the aid of the school to this end. That is, whether by deliberate design or unconscious ethnocentrism, it asserts the predominant value of its culture, and structures the school so as to reinforce its position and devalue that of others (Smolicz, 1979).

The role of the organizing authorities who carry out the policies of the dominant group is extremely important in that it is they who set the norms, determine the specific directives to be followed, monitor implementation, and define the organizational structure and climate of the school.

Too determinate a role in race and ethnic relations must not be accorded the dominant group, however; it is typically dominant within a system rather than over it. Single factor explanations, moreover, particularly those emphasizing the all-embracing determinacy of social class, are clearly incomplete.

Dominant–subordinate group relations are not carved in stone; indeed, they are frequently in a state of flux. That this is so is vividly demonstrated, for example, by the exceptional dynamism of the mass cultural market which has provoked issues of authority between traditional institutions (state, educational and religious) and market institutions (Williams, 1981). Frequently, too, dominant group interpretations of culture or attempts at managing interracial and intergroup relations are hotly contested. Such resistance is frequently located in the school and there are clear reasons why this is so. For what constitutes school knowledge and school achievement is a social and ethnic construct. And as such it assumes high importance in an achievement-oriented socially and ethnically stratified society.

While power-conflict approaches to the analysis of race and ethnic relations have much to offer, the field in general suffers from a number of important limitations that have a serious impact on the analysis of race relations and ethnic relations in education. For example, much of the theoretical literature, owing perhaps to the fact that ethnicity was originally conceived in terms of racial origin, discusses race relations and ethnic relations in tandem.

Too close an association between ethnicity and race has distinct analytical and practical disadvantages. In Australia it has resulted in ethnicity being equated with cultural differences; race meanwhile is ignored (Bullivant, 1984). In the Netherlands and the United Kingdom, educational policies based on models of cultural pluralism, which treat cultural and not racial differences, inadequately address issues of race and racism (Jones & Miedem, 1984).

In Canada, where concepts of race and ethnicity have been inter-preted differently over time, the problem is particularly acute. It is exacerbated by the existence of two distinct literatures (English and French) in which the concepts are also treated differently. In the nineteenth century, the concept of race was often used indistinguishably from concepts of ethnicity and nationality, particularly in the French–Canadian literature. Frequently, too, racism has been viewed as a subset of immigration problems (Wardaugh, 1983). This is not to suggest that historically Canadian immigration policies were not racist — clearly they were (Patel, 1980). Rather, it is to emphasize that, interpreting race relations solely from the point of view of immigration or cultural differences shifts attention away from considerations of race and racism. To do so is obviously an inadequate basis for policy development in general and educational policy in particular. Yet, historically, analyses of race relations in education have been tied closely to the education of immigrants (Brown, 1969). And a more recent study confirms that the issue of race continues to be framed within a cultural and ethnic context (Kormos, 1981–2).

A second major limitation of the race relations and ethnic relations literature is that insufficient recognition is given to the fact that these relations are part of a larger set of economic and political relations and are historically located. That is, they are constructed, enacted and managed within a particular context, one in which social formation and individual behaviour interact (Barton & Walker, 1983). It is in fact a major error to conceive of the conditions and problems of pluralism as being limited to a consideration of race relations and ethnic relations. To do so is to mistake the social myth for reality, and to miss the structure that underlies these relations and gives them both force and form (Smith, 1965). As a consequence, greater emphasis has been placed in the race relations literature on the 'deviant individual' perspective and the 'social forces perspective' to the virtual exclusion of the 'institutional-structural' perspective (Patel, 1980).

The 'deviant individual' perspective, as its label implies, views racism and racist behaviour as aberrant, pathological and restricted to the individual; it assumes that existing institutions can resolve problems fairly and peacefully. The 'social forces' perspective considers racism and racial problems as arising out of relatively impersonal social conditions such as migration and urban overpopulation. The 'institutional-structural' perspective, a more recent development, sees racism and responses to it as basically structural, purposeful and politically meaningful.

Analyses of racism and racial conflict have generally adopted the first two of the above three perspectives and seen them as isolated, mutually exclusive categories. Policy-makers have generally followed suit and as a consequence policy outcomes have been piecemeal, temporary and largely unsuccessful when viewed in terms of their declared goals. Yet, as Patel points out:

> Individuals and groups do not exist outside the social structure, which ultimately affects the relationships between groups and individuals through the various institutional orders and spheres. So the racism built into the Canadian structure from its very beginnings permeates the major social institutions and, through them, groups and individuals within Canadian society. Thus, for example, both the policeman or immigration officer and the unemployed, little-educated, or maladjusted youth have been socialized by the educational system, family, mass media, and so forth into Canadian beliefs (hence behaviour), which consider non-whites inferior and a threat. (1980: 46)

Furthermore, he continues, political considerations have usually pre-empted attempts to modify basic social structures and institutions, despite the obvious limitations involved in restricting changes to the level of the individual and/or social conditions. As a result, 'attempting to change the racist attitudes and behaviour of, say, individual teachers or policemen without changing the norms and roles of their respective institutional settings (e.g. schools and police departments) and related structures (e.g. the educational and justice systems), which govern the individual's attitudes and behaviour, would be like trying to change the nature of the game by changing the players but not the rules that govern the play' (Patel, 1980: 3).

Theories of schooling

The two major sociological theories employed in analyses of education are structural-functionalism (or consensus) theory and conflict (or power-conflict) theory. Structural-functionalism is the most widely applied of the two. It finds its basis in the work of nineteenth-century sociologists such as Emile Durkheim and was developed in its most recognizable form in the mid-twentieth century by Talcott Parsons (1959). Education, according to Durkheim, is essential to the survival of society and 'hence the elders feel the need to intervene, to bring about themselves the transmission of culture by epitomizing their experiences and deliberately passing on ideas, sentiments and knowledge from their minds to those of the young' (1973: 189). Viewed from this perspective moral and intellectual culture are too important to be left to chance. Societal needs must be met and societal structures reinforced. It is the function of the school to meet these needs and reinforce these structures. Correspondingly benefits to the individual flow from exposure to the society's collective culture heritage, which provides a sense of identity and belonging.

These ideas were developed further by Parsons, who based his ideas on the central notion that society is an integrated, interdependent whole, normally existing in a state of equilibrium. Institutions and structures were developed in order to meet society's basic needs and these needed to remain stable. Different needs naturally led to the establishment of institutions and structures which performed different functions. Educational institutions and structures, for example, according to Parsons, had two major functions: student internalization of basic societal values and the allocation of young people to adult roles. The most important adult roles were to be occupied by those who possessed the most talent and worked the hardest. Thus achievement, not ascription, was to be rewarded. Similarly, upward social mobility, based in large part upon open competition and educational qualifications, was endorsed on the grounds that it was essential to the future development of society. Not only did the concept of meritocracy provide a justification for the existence of a socio-economic hierarchy, but it also served to rationalize its counterpart, socio-economic inequality.

This view of society and its educational institutions resulted in the promotion of a competitive, individualistic philosophy in the schools, which were themselves organized to reinforce these values. Pupils learned to compete by competing for grades, prizes and awards, and were assessed and streamed on a continuous, on-going basis. At the high school and post-secondary levels of education, educational programs became more and more closely related to occupations and future occupational status. As differences among students emerged, the schools legitimated them on the grounds of equality of educational opportunity and open, meritocratic competition. Students frequently internalized these values and accepted the differences without complaint (Murphy, 1979). As a result, stability, equilibrium and consensus were reinforced.

The major intellectual source of many of the basic ideas contained in conflict or power-conflict theory is the work of Karl Marx and his followers. Marx saw industrial society as conflict-ridden because the opposed economic interests of the bourgeoisie and the proletariat did not admit of the possibility of consensus. Economics and economic relations shaped society and gave rise to an institutional superstructure (government, law, education, and so on) dominated by the ruling economic class. The function of this superstructure, including the educational system, was to promote the ideology of the dominant class and to preserve the *status quo*.

Change, on the other hand, was possible. It occurred precisely because of the opposed economic interests of the different classes and the conflicts to which they gave rise. In brief, then, conflict theory is based upon an assumption of opposed interests of groups in a society, rather than an assumption of consensual integration. It therefore 'promotes the search for contradictions and sources of disequilibrium in the system. Conflict is seen as the motor force of social changes.' (Murphy, 1979: 85)

Classical Marxists see the eventual demise of class conflict and the emergence of a classless, socialist state. Max Weber and adherents of his theoretical position, on the other hand, consider conflict to be a permanent feature of society. Weberians believe that in addition to economic interest groups, status groups, political parties and various other types of interest groups are also sources of antagonism and conflict. Moreover, conflict, they believe, can result from differences in ideals as well as in interests. According to them, societal structures and institutions have come into being to help resolve these conflicts. In attempting to do so, they in turn undergo change. Ideally, the checks and balances that structures and institutions are believed to possess mediate the struggles that take place within them. For later conflict theorists, however, the possession of power is the real key to the resolution of interest group struggles. Groups with power exert domination over those with less, hence much of the analysis in power-conflict is expressed in terms of the relationship between dominant and subordinate groups.

How have structural-functional and power-conflict theories of education been applied in Canada? An informed review of this question has been provided by Pike (1981) who observes that a general feature of functionalist theory is to view society as consisting of a relatively stable and persistent structure of elements. The function of these elements — the educational system for example — is to contribute towards the maintenance of the society as a whole. Functionalist writers, therefore, have tended to concentrate on the perceived functions of the educational system in society and

> have usually considered major educational change . . . as occurring in response to the requirements of the polity and the economy for more

highly educated citizens and workers. Conflict theory, on the other hand, tends to lay emphasis not upon social integration but rather upon such features of social life as conflict, coercion and the struggles for scarce resources. (Pike, 1981: 3)

The merging of economic theory and liberal doctrine during the post-war years in Canada found support from the functionalists who dominated English-Canadian sociology in that period. Many of them believed that the social stratification system, that is, differences in income, power and prestige among social groups, functions to attract the most ambitious and talented persons to the best-paid, most prestigious occupational positions. Thus, Pike observes,

they could certainly support an economic doctrine (human capital) which in alliance with a moral concept (equality of educational opportunity), appeared to offer the prospect of an increasingly good fit between top jobs and top talents. (Pike, 1981: 4)

Conflict theorists, on the other hand, questioned the opportunity for intergenerational social mobility through the educational system. Because the academic stratification system employed in high schools is also, to some extent, a social stratification system, they argued that the function of such a system may well result in 'dampening down the educational aspirations of those bright lower class students who tend, in relatively large numbers, to enrol in programmes which do not qualify them for university admission' (Pike, 1981: 9).

The most prominent post-war Canadian sociologist to analyse the relationship between the stratification system and the educational system was the late John Porter. In his major work, *The Vertical Mosaic: A Study of Class and Power in Canadian Society* (1965), he adopted to a considerable degree a functionalist view of the values of social mobility and individual achievement. School attainment, he believed, was an important resource for both the individual and society. Ethnicity, on the other hand, he saw as a barrier to the achievement of structural assimilation in that it emphasized traditional rather than future-oriented ways of life (1969). For Porter, class, not race or ethnicity, was the crucial variable, and the differences in power among social classes, not cultural or linguistic groups, was his major concern.

Because of his belief in the importance of class, and the power of the stratification system, Porter adopted a liberal assimilationist position in which he argued that ethnic group maintenance reduced the social and economic mobility of individuals. The choice facing Canadians, he wrote, was 'between the ethnic stratification that results from ethnic diversity and the greater possibilities for equality that result from a reduction of ethnicity as a salient feature of modern society' (1972: 205). For his part, despite some evidence of occasional misgivings, he came down in favour of the latter option.

Porter, however, was no uncritical exponent of structural-functionalism. He was well aware of the large gap that existed between the ideal of equal educational opportunity and its reality. He appreciated the fact that children from low-income homes were handicapped in the educational competition. He understood that money did indeed matter when it came to taking advantage of educational opportunity (Porter *et al.*, 1973). Like others (for example, Forcese & Richer, 1975) he was well aware that an important underlying feature of the social stratification system was the inegalitarian nature of the educational system (Denis and Murphy, 1977). Yet, while sensitive to the dilemmas and contradictions of a plural society, his analysis of Canadian society and its educational system is closer to the technical functionalism tradition than to conflict theory (Porter, 1981).

Clement (1975) has adopted a more conflict-oriented perspective than Porter in his analysis of the corporate élite and economic power in Canada. In particular, he distinguished between inequality of opportunity and inequality of condition. The former he defined as differential access to élite positions while the latter resulted from the hierarchically organized nature of Canadian society. Inequality of condition, he argued, leads to inequality of opportunity because the élite successfully transmit their privileges, inherited wealth, social contacts, and access to élite private educational institutions to their children. The children of the élite are therefore well-equipped in educational terms, but it is the initial advantages resulting from their social origins which put them in a privileged position to obtain this education. The public school system, on the other hand, he argued, teaches respect for élite culture, emphasizes educational requirements which reflect the interests of the élite, and serves as a screening device for identifying talented individuals to help renew and revitalize it (Murphy, 1979). The school, then, is not a neutral agency. It serves the ideology and interests of the dominant classes rather than those of subordinate groups. Implicitly, therefore, the school is a potential arena of conflict and struggle.

In Canada power-conflict theory has been seen as a valuable corrective to structural-functional analyses of society and education. It has demonstrated convincingly that Canadian society is stratified and that for some groups public education does not lead to upward social mobility. By relating existing institutions and structures to class or status group interests, moreover, it has provided a more meaningful and realistic analysis of Canadian society. Nevertheless, power-conflict theory (as is also the case with theories of structural-functionalism) is limited in its analysis of race and ethnicity in education.

Modern structural-functionalist theories of society have not placed much importance on the retention and support of minority ethnic cultures. Viewing society as a series of interdependent parts has meant that integration has considered the key goal. It followed from this that the function of the school was to emphasize common values; hence, the development of the deeply embedded notion of the public school as the 'common' school. This idea was firmly fixed in the people's consciousness and stressed the primacy of assimilation over diversity. Ethnicity therefore was assumed to be dysfunctional because it was believed it focused attention on ascriptive rather than achieved characteristics.

Classical Marxist theories of conflict frequently view ethnicity as an obstacle to the development of a classless, socialist state. Weberian conflict theorists just as frequently view ethnicity differences as being primarily economic in origin. Power-conflict theorists, on the other hand, view ethnic conflicts and their sources in broader terms. All three theoretical perspectives, however, emphasize that educational qualifications have not resulted in upward social mobility for members of certain racial and ethnic groups.

Ascriptive factors remain important for occupational placement and success. Society is built from status groups sharing a common culture, and groups are differentiated according to their positions of economic and cultural power. Dominant groups use education and élite educational institutions to socialize their own members into élite status, while at the same time using the public school system to socialize members of subordinate groups into according respect to dominant group values. Upper-class aspiring families avoid the public schools and send their offspring to schools tailored to their expectations and behavioural values. These schools are linked in turn first to élite institutions of higher eudcation and then to élite occupations. The public school system meanwhile legitimates middle and upper-class values and holds open the prospect of entry into these classes by hard-working, high-achieving youth from the working and lower-middle classes. In these and related ways, power-conflict theorists argue, the educational system works to maintain the interests of the dominant groups and the perpetuation of cultural and economic differences.

Both structural-functional and power conflict analyses of education have received their share of criticism, with advocates of each criticizing the other. This criticism is to be expected, given that the former stresses universalistic notions of values and schooling around which consensus is not only possible but achievable, while the latter emphasizes group differences, scarce resources and the existence of power differentials as causal points of conflict. Thus consensus theories of education have been attacked for paying insufficient attention to (or even ignoring) conflict; and conflict theories have been criticized for being overly deterministic, inflexible and unsuited to the analysis of specific educational contexts. Functionalists too have been censured for not accounting for race, class, ethnic and gender discrimination; conflict theorists for emphasizing class analyses to the detriment of an explanation involving variables of race, ethnicity and gender. Finally, both structural-functionalism and conflict theories of education have been characterized as macro-sociological theories that have neglected micro-sociological analyses of classroom, school and community settings (Murphy, 1979).

Conclusion

In the previous pages several bodies of theoretical literature have been examined from the perspective of schooling in plural societies and a number of important limitations identified. Pre-eminent among these is the fact that no comprehensive theory of schooling in plural societies is currently available. Where analyses of schooling in plural societies exist, for the most part they have been contained within the limited framework of normative and cultural pluralism. Rarely has schooling been examined in the context of socio-economic, political, institutional and structural forms of pluralism. Existing studies, moreover, have been conducted largely from the viewpoint of the majority or dominant group; studies undertaken from the point of view of minority or subordinate groups are virtually non-existent. Consequently, the contested nature of race relations and ethnic relations in education has been downplayed. Prevailing theories of schooling have stressed the school's role in cultural transmission and emphasized notions of neutrality, stability and consensus. Finally, it is with these limitations firmly in mind that an attempt is made in the following two chapters to develop the outlines of an alternative theoretical framework within which to analyze schooling in a plural Canada.

2 Contemporary forms of pluralism

Introduction

The most valuable macro-analysis of inter-group relations to be found in the theoretical literature in recent years is that provided by R. A. Schermerhorn in *Comparative Ethnic Relations: A Framework for Theory and Research* (1970). Observing that the central purpose of any general sociological theory is to postulate the essential nature of social interaction, he grounds his theory in the argument that inter-group relations are to be seen 'as a special case of societal relations in their broadest and most generic sense, rather than as a separate and unrelated field of inquiry' (p. 17). Consequently, in his effort to formulate a more adequate theory, he analyses societal formations in terms of whether they help either to foster integration or to stimulate conflict.

The two major theoretical approaches examined in the preceding chapter, structural-functionalism and power-conflict theory, are examined and found wanting. The former, Schermerhorn argues, suffers from the proclivity of functionalists and systems analysts to emphasize symmetrical relationships — a preference that has led them to place a selective emphasis on congruence, mutuality, complementarity and organic balance. Structural functionalists adopt the view that societies can only persist as and when total system needs are satisfied. Priority is accorded to these needs, and structures established which are characterized by stability and predictability. Their primary function is maintenance of the existing system. Whether they are good or bad in terms of individual preferences or partial group standards is less important. Not surprisingly, therefore, this approach has generally worked to support preservation of the *status quo*.

Power-conflict theory, Schermerhorn notes, is based on the concept of inherent scarcity of means. Attempts to control these means result in open or concealed conflicts requiring the application of power to attain and maintain control. Efforts to resolve these conflicts result in the development of unequal power relations. These relations, however, are not fixed, and continued contestation of control leads to emphasis being placed on change rather than preservation of the *status quo*. Societal institutions and structures reflect this emphasis. They are more open to modification and are frequently characterized as being more pluralistic, flexible and accommodating. However, conflicts between groups of unequal power, Schermerhorn points out, are not necessarily destabilizing. They can also engender integrative bonds which possess system characteristics of their own (Schermerhorn, 1970: 53).

Despite a declared preference for power-conflict analyses Schermerhorn does not recommend dispensing altogether with structural-functionalism or systems analysis. This approach he describes as tantamount to casting ourselves 'adrift on a sea of ceaseless flux with only the waves to guide us' (1970: 33, 34). Rather he considers the two theoretical approaches to be alternatives that have greater or lesser relevance at different points in his analysis. They are not in his view dichotomous intellectual systems, nor for explanatory purposes must an either/or choice be made. Dialectical analysis, the sociological approach Schermerhorn advocates, has no essential incompatibility with either theory; it cuts across both.

Adoption of this approach possesses three mutually reinforcing advantages. First, it keeps the analyst face to face with the concrete realities of social situations, underlines their fluidity and complexity, and serves to correct the one-sidedness of narrow explanations. Second, the dialectical approach does not bolster any particular ideological position; it is 'a weapon that can be used against all ideologies, an empirical sort of probing that asks whether unsuspected dualities are lurking in our answers — sometimes leading to affirmative, sometimes to negative replies' (1970: 49). And third, it makes an important analytical distinction between culture and structure. For Schermerhorn:

> Culture signifies the ways of action learned through socialization, based on norms and values that serve as guides or standards for that behaviour. Social structure, on the other hand, refers to 'the set of crystallized social relationships which its (the society's) members have with each other which places them in groups, large or small, permanent or temporary, formally organized or unorganized, and which relates them to the major institutional activities of the society, such as economic and occupational life, religion, marriage and the

family, education, government and recreation. Culture has to do with standards or 'designs for living' while social structure refers to the clustering of men in patterned ways which may or may not be regulated by the overarching norms and values. Of course this is not a complete dichotomy but a dialectical relation in which each aspect of the social whole interacts with the other. Values and norms often defined the human groupings and institutions that circumscribe man's conduct, while on the other hand, man's actions give rise to new or changed values and standards (1970: 80).

The importance of adopting a dialectical approach to the analysis of schooling is reinforced when it is recognized that education is a scarce resource and that attempts to control it frequently result in open or concealed conflict in which power differentials are wielded by groups to achieve selective ends. That dominant groups wield greater power and influence over schools than do subordinate groups is clear. This is reflected, for example, in the governance, administration and content of public schooling, and is particularly marked in terms of educational outcomes among working-class and racial minorities. Moreover, these examples are not self-subsistent phenomena, for they obviously take their shape from the social organization and directional processes in which they occur (Schermerhorn, 1970). Thus, educational processes are inextricably related to tensions and conflicts in the larger society. As such they need to be seen as occurring in a context shaped by more general economic, political and social conditions. For as two British scholars have pointed out:

> If we are to speak with assurance about issues like the origins of community conflict, the nature of racism, the constraints upon the conditions of schooling, social policy and community care provided for a multiracial society, then we need a more developed exploration of the political, social and economical provision and practices. (Barton & Walker, 1983)

Finally, by adopting a dialectical approach to analyses of schooling in a plural society, the intimate relationship between culture and politics is reinforced, and the interlocking roles of symbols (the language of instruction, for example) and power revealed (Singleton, 1977).

A second major contribution made by Schermerhorn consists of the analytical differences he makes between different forms of pluralism: cultural, normative, political and structural. Cultural pluralism, the form of pluralism most often invoked in connection with schooling, refers to the presence of racial and ethnic groups possessing languages and/or other cultural norms and values which differentiate them from the dominant group in a society. Normative pluralism, usually expressed in ideological terms, refers to the realm of goals and objectives such as the toleration or appreciation of cultural differences. Political pluralism refers to the existence of a multiplicity of autonomous groups and associations (including but not restricted to those possessing an ethnocultural base) that exert pressure on the initiation, formulation, and implementation of public policy. Structural pluralism refers to the presence of institutions and structures reflecting racial and cultural diversity. These range from a situation where complete duplication of services is provided to a situation where racial and ethnic groups participate in a number of common institutions, but also continue to maintain those which reflect their own distinctive cultural features. A fifth form, socio-economic pluralism, while not explicitly cited by Schermerhorn, is implicit in his work. Its importance with respect to the analysis of schooling in a plural society is crucial.

Cultural pluralism

Cultural pluralism is an imprecise concept and one that is rather loosely employed in the literature on pluralism. Some difficulty has been experienced also in defining it in the literature on education in plural societies (Gibbons, 1976). Most writers who employ the concept, however, consider it goes beyond objective cultural differences (Van den Berghe, 1973). Thus an early version in the United States, for example, interpreted cultural pluralism as being based on the claim that the culture of an immigrant nation would be enhanced if it preserved the best values of each ethnic group (Payne, 1937). Similarly, it has been considered that the adoption of a policy of cultural pluralism meant there was no need to sacrifice one's ethnic identity. Group relationships were ordered in such a way as to avoid extremes of inequality and each group felt it was obtaining benefit from association in the common society (Hunt and Walker, 1974). Another version saw cultural pluralism as involving at least the minimal acceptance of dominant beliefs by minority groups. And yet other versions have considered policies of cultural pluralism to be dysfunctional (Wardaugh, 1983) or to be likely to obscure more important social problems (Bullivant, 1981).

The concept is used frequently without benefit of definition in Canada. According to McLeod (1979a), since no ethnic group forms an outright majority, and since neither Anglo- nor Franco-Canadians settled and developed the land in certain regions, cultural pluralism has been considered a suitable social and cultural policy for Canadians, albeit one that has frequently been ignored (Wardaugh, 1983). For present purposes, however, cultural pluralism can be defined as the presence of ethnic groups whose language, religion and/or other traditional norms and values are embodied in patterns that set them off from the dominant group. Five major periods of settlement, for example, have exercised a profound impact on the racial and cultural composition of Canada's population. The first, the pre-European period, extended over ten thousand years and led to scattered occupation of the territory by the racially, culturally and linguistically heterogeneous aboriginal peoples. The second coincided with the period of French colonization up until 1760. The third followed the ceding of French-Canada to Britain at the *Treaty of Paris* (1763), and was characterized by the arrival of large numbers of British immigrants. As a result, Anglophones outnumbered Francophones by the middle of the nineteenth century. The fourth period coincided to a large extent with the settlement and development of the Prairie Provinces. This resulted in the addition of immigrants from non-Anglophone and non-Francophone ethnocultural and linguistic backgrounds (Germans, Ukrainians and Icelanders, to name a few). The fifth is a much more recent phenomenon and occurred as a consequence of the opening up of entry to Canada to large numbers of immigrants from the Caribbean, Asia, Africa and South America.

Normative or ideological pluralism

The ideological system, since it coordinates and structures all other cultural and social systems, has been described as the most vital element of a society's culture. Normative ideologies, moreover, are a fundamental part of every society and serve as important sources of cohesion and unity. In federal societies, normative or ideological pluralism is a widely acknowledged principle, one that is based on the premise that all groups that continue to interact with each other develop normative regularities and system interdependencies (Schermerhorn, 1970). A principal function of an ideological system is to act as an evaluating agent. That is, it assesses the significance of new values by comparing them with existing standards and norms of conduct. Consequently, ideological systems also bear within them the potential to respond to changing needs and circumstances (Smolicz, 1979).

In Canada, for example, normative or ideological pluralism is a widely acknowledged principle of government. Canadian federalism, it has been argued, developed in large part because it made

> possible the large political and economic unit required to sustain genuine political independence and to facilitate rapid economic development while at the same time assuming the varied linguistic, racial and religious communities some autonomy. (Watts, 1970: 1)

The ideal of 'unity within diversity' has served as a prime normative goal aimed at providing significant cultural minorities with an enduring sense of distinctiveness and generating a sense of community among diverse groups (Watts, 1970: 28). Normative ideals are the basic 'software' of politics. But, despite their importance, they have rarely been the subject of critical scrutiny (Michael, 1983). Even more rarely have the normative goals of educational systems, whose role in the stabilization of ideological systems is widely appreciated, been assessed (Smolicz, 1979). Yet ideologies are routinely expressed in educational policies. The latter are primarily a set of ideas and beliefs about society, located in concrete educational practices (Giroux, 1983b), that exert considerable influence over individuals and groups. It is especially true that the dominant ideology significantly shapes the culture and structure of public schooling.

Normative statements also have been described as ideal future claims (Bullivant, 1981). Hence, when contrasted with the monocultural conformity of many school systems, they underline the point 'that the ideological field in any given society is saturated with contradictions within and between ... emerging, residual and dominant ideologies' (Giroux, 1983b: 146). These ideologies, of course, can either distort or illuminate reality, and may be accepted or resisted. Resistance to the dominant ideology, for example, occurs when its normative values are not matched by performance. Conflicts result and, when viewed in the context of specific struggles, ideologies frequently illuminate relations among interests, knowledge and power. They possess particular potential for the analysis of the intimate relationship that exists between power and the organization and structure of schooling.

Institutional and structural pluralism

The links between the forms of pluralism discussed above and their institutional and structural expression have been largely inferred to this point. It is now time to examine them more closely. The closest links exist between cultural and structural pluralism. According to Schermerhorn (1970: 124)

> culture and social structure are virtual Siamese twins, with each implicated in the other. So if a cultural group has its own special set of norms, they will *ipso facto* define certain institutions or patterns that separate the members of that group structurally from adjacent groups, at least in some minimal way.

Multiethnic societies, therefore, are by implication societies that possess plural institutions and structures. They vary widely, however, ranging from societies where the monopoly of power is exercised by a single dominant group (frequently regulating subordinate ethnic groups through coercive political institutions), to those where subordinate ethnic groups participate in a number of institutional orders while maintaining their distinctive cultural features. Depending upon the relationship between dominant and subordinate groups, subordinate racial and ethnic groups experience greater or lesser institutional enclosure (Schermerhorn, 1970). A broad spectrum of institutional and structural differentiation, for example, may be observed with dividing lines ranging from complete ascription of group membership (with a corresponding lack of mobility from one group to another) to loosely formed groups where the dividing lines have either failed or are breaking down (Van den Berghe, 1973). These various types of institutional and structural differentiation, moreover, do not only constitute analytical categories. They also reflect, in concrete form, the different degrees of power, authority, wealth and knowledge possessed by dominant and subordinate ethnic groups. Together they define and constitute the societal framework in which they are found (Smith, 1965).

The importance of analyzing institutional and structural pluralism in racially and culturally diverse societies has long been recognized. Smith (1965) holds that the core of a culture is its institutional system. And, since society consists of a system of institutionalized relations, the different institutional forms together make up its social, political and economic structures. Certain racial and ethnic groups exercise dominant control over these structures, and the status of a subordinate group's culture relates directly to its status in the economic and political structure (Bullivant, 1981: 72). An ethnic group's cultural vitality, especially its linguistic vitality, is closely related to the degree of institutional support it enjoys (Bourhis, 1984). For these and related reasons then, it is essential for a sociology of culture to concern itself

with the analysis of institutions and of the forms of cultural production
they promote and legitimize (Williams, 1981).

Other analysts argue for locating the analysis of institutional and
structural change formally in the context of conflicting power relations.
They see structures as waystations, a temporary halt between opposing
forces of modally unequal power, containing and regularizing conflict
between interest groups (without actually eliminating them) until such
conflict engenders new structures (Schermerhorn, 1970). They recognize
the importance of struggle against the structures of domination and stress
the fact that structures are shaped in part by forms of resistance (Willis,
1983). Struggle and resistance, it is argued, promote the development of
oppositional historical consciousness (Giroux, 1981). Institutions are not
disembodied phenomena but emergent individuals or groups of individuals
(Livingstone, 1983).

These theories, as we shall see in the next chapter, have exercised
some influence in current analyses of education. Indeed, the recent work
of critical theorists of schooling can be said to have made a significant
contribution to the larger debate. Apple (1979), for example, believes
that the educational system occupies a central position in society's
network of cultural institutions and structures. It is no accident,
therefore, that democrats point out the danger of educational institutions over which participants have no control, or that they stress the
need for structures that are supportive of participatory democracy
(Itzkoff, 1969). Nor should we be surprised to hear of demands for more
freedom of choice in educational systems (Lynch & Plunkett, 1973);
calls for the decentralization of schooling along cultural lines; or
expressions of support for curricula that reflect the realities of culturally
differentiated contexts (Singleton, 1977). If these interests go unmet, or
if they are only grudgingly recognized, then conflict is likely to occur. It
should be stressed, for example, that conflicts over racism in schools and
local communities 'are not simple products of isolated episodes or of
individual interpretations and whims, rather they are rooted in the
well-established and deeply entrenched institutional routines of group
life' (Barton & Walker, 1983: 8). Our analyses, therefore, must be
conducted at the group and institutional as well as individual levels (Van
den Berghe, 1973). We must go beyond the reductionism of base-
superstructure formulas to study the complex sociology of inter-group
relations, institutions and structures located in their changing historical
context. And, finally, our analyses of institutional and structural
pluralism in education must be measured against the socio-political
arrangements in the larger society (Giroux, 1981).

Political pluralism

Political pluralism traditionally refers to the multiplicity of autonomous groups and associations, including those possessing a racial and ethno-cultural base, that bring pressure to bear on the development and implementation of political decisions. Historically, unity in diversity has tended in many people's minds to be treated synonymously with that of democratic pluralism, although others have questioned the compatibility of a democratic political organization with a capitalist order of economic production.

Ideally, autonomous pressure groups and the web of private links citizens have with the family, neighbourhood and voluntary associations, serve to mediate between the individual and the state (Townsend, 1983). In addition to preventing the state 'or even any private source of power from gaining monopolistic weight, they help to train citizens in the political skills necessary for carrying on the democratic process; they accustom men to accept the legitimacy of opposition' (Schermerhorn, 1970: 123). For with some oversimplification, it can be said that within any political environment, policies are formulated on two bases: the perception of the situation by government officials and the pressure exerted by interest groups (Weiss, 1983). The latter, it should be noted, are pressure groups and not governing mechanisms (Leary, 1983).

Among political analysts there is a widespread belief that ethnicity, not class, is the basis of political mobilization and action. Nevertheless, especially in the western industrial nations, the role that ethnicity has taken in politics over the last three decades has occasioned some surprise (Glazer & Moynihan, 1975). Few have attempted to explain why ethnicity is such a potent base for political mobilization, and why ethnic politics are so attractive. In part, the potency of ethnicity lies in the fact that it is both an expressive and an instrumental pattern of action (Singleton, 1977). On the other hand, however, such universalistic explanations must be tempered by specific local conditions and circumstances.

Issues concerning ethnicity and culture have long played a dominant role in the political debate in Canada. And while the French–English conflict is central to this debate, in recent years it has been broadened to embrace concerns expressed by the so-called 'third force' — that is, those racial, cultural and linguistic groups who see themselves as belonging to neither the Francophone nor the Anglophone communities.

Just how significant this 'third force' may be is itself a matter of some debate. It has been suggested (but not fully documented) that members of the 'third force' are increasingly occupying important offices at various levels in municipal, provincial and national politics and that the number of elected representatives from their ranks is also growing (Boissevain, 1970). Other analysts, however, dispute this reading of the situation (Moodley, 1983); they deem the 'third force' to be an insignificant political power at the federal level (Wardaugh, 1983), point to the absence of formal policies of multiculturalism among political parties, and consider the base for further political action largely to have disappeared (Lupul, 1983). As one commentator has it, 'in Canada the dominant political culture suggests that the "other" ethnic people can become fully Canadian if they fulfil certain obligations, most notably not to cling to foreign cultures as living wholes' (Peter, 1981: 57). These differences in opinion emphasize the extent to which the impact of race, ethnicity and culture on Canadian political pluralism is in a state of dynamic flux. This is particularly the case with respect to issues of public schooling.

All public schooling is in its practice and implications a political process, and therefore inseparable from the political and economic context in which it is offered. And, as politics is the pre-eminent process whereby societal and group ideas are integrated, such integration necessarily involves considerations of power and its organization. Traditionally, however, most political scientists who have focused on education have confined their analyses to the study of educational politics rather than the politics of education. In doing so, they have consciously or unconsciously bracketed out political questions and replaced them with questions about processes of decision-making and administration. The emphasis has been placed 'on the machinery, rather than on what powers it has or how and where it is directed' (Dale *et al.*, 1982: 128–9). Traditionally, too, research on education in plural societies has conceived of politics and school systems intersecting at but one major point: the socialization of ethnic minorities to the dominant culture (Wirt, 1979). Or, to put it in the terms in which it is usually expressed, research in education has dealt with ethnicity in the context of concerns for nation-building. That is, ethnicity has been seen as a categorical reference rather than a political process, while ethnic groups have been treated implicitly as static systems constraining the political integration of nations (Singleton, 1977).

These traditional approaches have not gone without notice or criticism in multiracial, multicultural societies where activities centred around race and ethnicity have assumed new and heightened political profiles. The scale, intensity and persistence of these new and dynamic forms of collective activity constitute a new level of politicization of public education, in which the struggle over its constituent values and their

allocation within the system possesses long-term implications and consequences (Lynch & Plunkett, 1973). This in turn has led to calls for a
statement of the theoretical relationship between the political system and
school policy as they affect cultural integration (Wirt, 1979), and between
multicultural education and the political framework within which it
operates and by which it is conditioned (Mitter, 1984). This means looking
at schools, according to one prominent critic,

> not only with reference to their existing connections with other
> agencies in the fields of production and cultural production, it also
> means tracing historically the ever-changing pattern of connections
> . . . By historically grounding the fight for control of schooling among
> competing political and socio-economic forces and their ac-
> companying educational theories, radical educational theory provides
> the framework for a viable strategy for radical educational reform.
> The strength of this framework lies in its usefulness in illuminating not
> only the contradictions that exist in the system of schooling but also
> the political interests which it legitimates and the ideologies which it
> perpetuates. (Giroux, 1981: 80)

In Canada, calls for alternative theoretical frames and analyses which
focus on the relationship between race, ethnicity and the politics of
schooling are being heard and acted upon. Thus, for example, Moodley
(1983: 326) has drawn attention to the presence of unequal ethnic life
chances, and called for multicultural education to be politicized in order
to improve the chances for school success of children from immigrant and
ethnocultural minority backgrounds. Similarly, Martel (1984), in her
comparison of the goals of second language programs, has expressed
interest in the question of whose interests are served by the present power
structure in education. Elsewhere, too, interest in the political analysis of
schooling has been expressed (Young, 1987). However, as we shall see in
Part Two of this text, actual practice continues to operate far in advance
of research and substantive theory in the politics of education. Much work
remains to be done.

Socio-economic pluralism

Socio-economic pluralism is the most important contemporary form of
pluralism to be examined in any analysis of schooling. It is the most
important because it is the outcome of interactions among the other forms
of pluralism. In sociological literature, socio-economic pluralism is usually

discussed in terms of ethnic stratification and social stratification. Social stratification is best understood as the division of society into broad strata forming a hierarchy of prestige, wealth and power. While no general theory of ethnic stratification exists, social and ethnic stratification are frequently treated as though they were virtually synonymous (Shibutani & Kwan, 1965). Alternatively, racial and ethnic stratification are subsumed under social stratification. These forms of reductionism are not without problems, however. Not only are racial, ethnic and social stratification systems analytically distinct, but the tendency to subsume them under the one heading of social stratification also mistakes (even ignores) the character and implications of institutional differentiation (Smith, 1965). This same tendency underestimates the very real disparities in power among racial and ethnic groups (Smooha, 1978) and downplays the significance of racism and ethnocentrism (Duberman, 1976).

The reverse tendency to overemphasize cultural differences to the detriment of analyses of socio-economic differences must also be avoided. The reality is that ethnic stratification and social stratification are intimately related. However, our understanding of the complexities of their relationship remains opaque.

Studies of the relationship between ethnic and social stratification in Canada are of relatively recent origin. Understandably, perhaps even the broad outlines are subject to fairly wide-ranging discussion and inter-pretation. Porter (1965), in his ground-breaking, macro-sociological study *The Vertical Mosaic: An Analysis of Social Class and Power in Canada*, considered the social stratification system to be based on the perpetuation of power by vested interest groups; ethnicity, moreover, was a principal factor in both its formation and persistence. He located the origin of the "vertical mosaic" in the power differentials that were established between the British and the French, the two ethnic groups first to settle the country. The British by virtue of conquest first assumed a position of superiority over the French and then assigned 'entrance status' to later immigrants on the basis of race, ethnicity and country of origin. The least assimilable groups were assigned the lowest status. Assigned positions in the social hierarchy, Porter argued (except in the case of the French), persisted over time and resulted in the formation of a vertical mosaic.

> Germans, Scandinavians and Dutch are the nearest to the British in their occupational level . . . . Italians, Polish, Ukrainians and groups from southeast Europe are still at the lower end of the occupational spectrum. The French could be placed somewhere between these last and the groups from northern Europe. (Porter, 1965: 90)

Native Indians and the Inuit occupied the lowest levels of the social stratification system (Porter, 1965: 562–564). Forcese (1980), on the other hand, while agreeing with Porter's rank ordering of ethnic groups and its persistence, is of the view that Canada possesses not one but two systems of stratification. The first is based on differences in social, economic and political power irrespective of ethnic background, the second on differences which exist precisely because the population is divided along lines of race, ethnicity and national origin.

Additional empirical evidence confirming the persistent nature of Canada's stratification system was furnished by Clement (1975). Clement concluded that, subsequent to Porter's collection of data, the class structure had crystallized as society matured, mobility had been stifled, and membership in the élite group had become even more concentrated, exclusive and powerful. Those of British ancestry remained firmly in place at the apex of the vertical mosaic (86.2%), while the French (8.4%) and members of the other ethnic groups (5.4%) were severely underrepresented. Clement's work also offered an important new insight into the nature of Canadian inequality. He drew a distinction between inequality of opportunity and inequality of condition. The latter he defined in terms of the class structure within which society was framed; the former as the freedom of persons with particular social, ethnic or economic characteristics to move within institutional settings created by the social structure. Inequality of condition, he observed, parallels the class structure and leads to inequality of opportunity. This process resulted from those who held dominant positions in the social structure accumulating power and privileges in the form of wealth, social position, influential contacts, and enhanced access to educational resources.

Relationships between ethnicity, social class and education are even less clear and certainly less well-researched than relationships between ethnic and social stratification. These, however, are intimately connected to a set of assumptions closely associated with theories of the liberal-democratic state. In the latter, it is assumed both that rewards are distributed on the basis of merit, and that the institutions and structures of democratically-elected governments function to reduce inequalities among individuals and groups. This is the predominant view taken of the function of the educational system. Education should be open to all who possess the desire and the ability to pursue it. Equality of educational opportunity, it is believed, will *ipso facto* lead to reductions of inequality. It is also believed that the expansion of equality of educational opportunity is fair, efficient and beneficial — fair in that the educational competition is open equally to all who possess talent and are prepared to develop it;

efficient in that the competition identifies and helps prepare appropriately qualified personnel to meet societal needs; beneficial in that individuals can choose careers on the basis of ability and interest. Hence, as educational attainment is judged to be the best predictor of future occupational level, social mobility based on merit is made possible. The school system, moreover, is considered to be both objective and neutral. Race, ethnicity and social class in this scheme of things are judged to exert little or no influence on educational outcomes.

Criticisms of liberal-democratic theories of education are not difficult to find. Bowles & Gintis (1976), for example, maintain the view that the educational system is so closely tied to the economic system that it functions to reproduce existing structures and patterns of inequality. Large-scale, centralized school reforms aimed at reducing differences in children's academic achievement have been shown to be inadequate and their ability to reduce inequalities have been documented (Karabel & Halsey, 1977). As Glazer & Moynihan (1975) have suggested, ethnicity may well be shown to be as important a phenomenon as social class in determining educational outcomes and, by extension, one's position in the socio-economic hierarchy. In Canada, criticisms of liberal-democratic theories of schooling and their relationship to racial, ethnic and social stratification can be illustrated by again examining the work of Porter & Clement. Both are critical of the belief that Canadian society is a meritocracy, or that its educational system provides equal opportunity for all, or that individuals are equally rewarded for hard work and ability. Both, too, have concluded that the educational system helps preserve the *status quo*.

Among other factors, Porter (1965) argues that ethnicity, financial inequalities, and regional disparities in educational access serve as barriers to full educational opportunity. The reproduction of inequalities takes place in part because differences in occupational distribution and income among ethnic groups lead to differential access to an inegalitarian educational system for their children. This process in turn shapes their occupational distribution and income in such a way as to reproduce existing inequalities. And so the pattern repeats itself. Clement, like Porter, recognizes that educational access, particularly to higher educa- tion, is largely restricted to the middle and upper classes. The élite are much better equipped to send their children to private fee-paying schools that possess close links to high-ranking public universities. Thus, given the relationship between educational attainment and the occupational struc- ture, these institutions serve as important screening devices that effectively exclude members of lower socio-economic groups from highly-skilled, highly-remunerative positions. The public secondary schools perform a similar function in that they screen out poor and working-class children before they get to university (Clement, 1975: 267). Clement is sceptical, therefore, that educational reforms can bring about fundamental structural change in the absence of more widespread economic and political change. The latter must precede educational reform because 'inequalities in economic condition lead to inequalities in educational opportunity which in turn are transformed into further economic inequalities' (Murphy, 1979: 117).

A third critic, Forcese (1980) also believes formal educational institutions serve as 'gatekeepers' that favour the already privileged, screen out the disadvantaged, and perpetuate an increasingly rigid stratification system. They do so, moreover, because their curriculum, teaching methods and expectations are geared to the needs and culture of the middle and upper classes. Schools function in two ways to reproduce ascribed inequalities from generation to generation. First, because of the inequalities of condition which children bring to school, and secondly, because the school reinforces the cultural capital possessed by the middle and upper classes. That is, children from these classes possess an initial advantage which is further reinforced throughout their years in school. They also benefit from the fact that their parents are much more familiar with the school system and are keenly aware of the significance of program choices for subsequent entry to higher education and future careers (Murphy, 1979). Children from low income groups, on the other hand, are placed at a disadvantage because of their cultural difference from the socially-determined culture of the school, its prescribed knowledge content and its social and linguistic codes that are so influential in the process of educational and ultimately social selection (Bernstein, 1971).

Research on these and related issues in Canada is recent, piecemeal, localized and incomplete. What research has been done, however, suggests a less clear-cut set of relationships than is argued in the macro-sociological literature cited above. Two types of findings are reported: those expressed in aggregate form and those presented by ethnic group. Among the former, findings drawn from a secondary analysis of data compiled on Ontario high school students in the late 1950s and early 1960s revealed that students from Canada's non-official language groups possessed the highest graduation rates irrespective of gender and father's occupation and educational background. A similar finding was obtained regarding plans to attend university (King & Angi, n.d.). A decade or so later Anisef (1975), analysing data on the impact of ethnicity of educational plans for grade 12 students in Ontario, found that a statistically

greater proportion of students with fathers born outside Canada expected
to enrol in university. A third study conducted by Traub *et al.* (1976)
examined the academic performance and educational intentions of Ontario
secondary school students and found that membership in the ethnic
minority did not affect scores in English and mathematics, and appeared
to encourage plans for additional education.

Findings of research which distinguishes between specific ethnicities
also throws new light on the findings of macro-sociological research and
provides further insight into the relationship of ethnicity, social class and
educational achievement. For example, a study carried out in the late
1960s in Ontario examined differences in educational achievement among
fifth-grade boys from five ethnic groups: Canadian Indian, Franco-
Ontarian, Jewish, West Indian and White Anglo-Saxon Protestant. One
of its major finds was that the scores for children from these groups
differed significantly on both the mental ability tests and the measures of
home learning environment employed in the study (Marjoribanks, 1970).
A second study carried out by the City of Toronto Board of Education in
the mid-1970s found a strong relationship between socio-economic status
and enrolment in pre-university programs. Considerable differences,
however, almost irrespective of socio-economic status existed when the
data was broken down by ethnic group. Students from Chinese, Ukrainian
and German backgrounds were most likely to be enrolled in pre-university
programs while students from French, Italian and Portuguese backgrounds
were least likely to be enrolled in them (Deosoran *et al.*, 1976).

A third and one of the most ambitious pieces of research in this area
also draws attention to the existence of differences among racial and ethnic
groups on measures of educational attainment (Herberg, 1980). In this
case, too, the influence of socio-economic factors varied according to
social, ethnic and religious background. The study examined census data
on the educational attainment of adults between 1951 and 1971 and the
educational attendance of students aged fifteen to twenty at formal
educational institutions among thirteen groups in five major cities. The
thirteen groups were identified as blacks, British, Chinese, East Indian,
French, German, Greek, Italian, Japanese, Jewish, Portuguese,
Scandinavian and Ukrainian; the five cities were Halifax, Montreal,
Toronto, Winnipeg and Vancouver. Based on analysis of the data, five
conclusions were reached and they are provided here in somewhat
abbreviated form:

1.   The position of each ethno-racial-religious group in the 1971 adult
     educational hierarchy in Canada differs considerably from that

obtained in 1951. The British, French and several of the other larger established ethnic groups have been displaced at the top of the 'educational ladder' by the visible minorities, the Jews and, probably, the Ukrainians.

2. Comparisons of youth attendance standings with those pertaining to adult educational attainment suggest that changes in the educational status of ethnic groups have continued during the 1970s.

3. Very great differences can be observed in educational attainment among ethnic groups in the same city; the relative value placed on formal education appears to vary greatly among ethnicities within the same social environment, suggesting that education fulfills very different functions in some groups from those in others.

4. Each ethnic group — and likely each one in each city — seems to be characterized by a unique set of internal social values and relations influencing the functions of formal education within that group in its social-geographic context.

5. Because function and accessibility from the perspective of ethnic groups varies by city, group and period, no fixed generalizations can be applied to them all (Herberg, 1984).

Given this degree of relativity and the limited nature of current research, one can only express the most tentative conclusions on 'group specific' relationships as between educational attainment, ethnic and social stratification. Yet while our understanding remains opaque, certain observations can be made. Sufficient evidence is available, for example, to indicate that the relationship varies between groups. Moreover, as Walberg & Marjoribanks (1976) suggest, correlational or causal relationships established for one group may not hold for other times or ethnic groups. There is also evidence to the effect that the 'vertical mosaic' is not as fixed and rigid as some authors have suggested. Certain groups but not others (such as the native peoples) have attained a considerable degree of upward mobility and have entered the middle level of the social stratification system. Why this is so and what role formal schooling plays in maintaining and modifying the continuing hierarchical nature of Canadian socio-economic pluralism remains unclear. Theories of cultural deprivation in which children who were culturally different were assumed to be culturally deficient are clearly inadequate and inappropriate in a plural society. The same can be said for the biological determinist theory which places the blame for low achievement on the child or the family. Deficit models simply do not explain the educational and socio-economic mobility that certain groups enjoy. We must look further, therefore, for explanatory theory and the findings of research. One potentially fruitful area is the examination of the cultural gap that exists for many children between the school and home (Lambert & Klineberg, 1967). Individual and group ambivalence towards the language of the home and that of the school may well be a factor underlying the poor achievement of many native groups (Cummins, 1984). This notion of 'bicultural ambivalence' is consistent with the work done by Ogbu (1978) documenting the need to go beyond linguistic or school program variables in explaining differences in the patterns of school performance of minorities. His structural analysis of severe failure among certain groups is suggestive and may profitably be linked to larger theories of social and economic change.

Research needs to go on at these levels. On the one hand, macro-sociological research is needed to more fully appreciate the relationship between the structures of the educational system and those of the economy and polity. Micro-sociological studies, on the other hand, are equally important if we are better to understand the links between the internal processes of the school and its structures. The third level may well prove to be the most crucial, however. This is research that symbolically links the two previous levels together, for structure and process are inextricably joined. That there has been a recognition of this central fact seems evident in the increasingly political involvement of minority groups seeking institutional and structural change in education.

Conclusion

In this chapter the literature on contemporary forms of pluralism have been examined with a view to identifying theoretical approaches possessing potential explanatory value. The importance of adopting a dialectical approach to the analysis of schooling is emphasized as is the intimate relationship between culture and politics. The approach cuts across power-conflict and structural-functionalist approaches, draws attention to the concrete realities of social situations, avoids particular ideological positions, and reinforces the analytical distinction between culture and structure.

The analytical differences between different forms of pluralism are stressed and their importance in the analysis of schooling in a plural society confirmed. Normative expressions of pluralistic ideals, especially their acceptance, rejection and translation into policy and practice, provide insight into the close relationship between groups' possession or lack of power and the content and organization of educational systems. The analytical categories of institutional and structural pluralism reflect the different degrees of power and authority possessed by dominant and subordinate groups in promoting and legitimizing different elements of culture by way of schooling. Political pluralism, or in this context the existence of autonomous groups and associations possessing a racial, linguistic and ethnic base, focuses our attention on the politics of education and the ways in which its processes perpetuates certain forms and content of schooling.

Finally, socio-economic pluralism, most frequently discussed in terms of ethnic and social stratification, locates the existence and persistence of power differentials between racial, linguistic and ethnic groups, and their influence on schooling in society's social and economic structures. Conclusive findings on the relationships between ethnicity, social class and education is lacking, however. Only tentative conclusions can be expressed on 'group specific' relationships between educational attainment, ethnic and social stratification. Much more empirical research obviously needs to be done incorporating both macro- and micro-sociological studies if we are to comprehend the impact of the social, economic and political systems on schooling in plural societies. In the interim, meanwhile, the literature on what is usually referred to as the new sociology of education provides valuable theoretical concepts that can help frame our studies. It is to an examination of this literature that we turn in the chapter that follows.

3 The new sociology of education

Introduction

Beginning in the 1960s and assuming momentum in the 1970s, a fairly comprehensive critique of existing sociological theories of education can be identified (Apple, 1978). The literature expanding this critique draws from more broadly based critical theory (Giroux, 1983) and reflects a growing commitment to critical pedagogy in which theory is more fully grounded in the day-to-day practices of schooling (Simon, 1983). It is an evolving literature that focuses on the socio-political and economic aspects of education (Olson, 1981), expresses considerable scepticism about theories of the school as a liberating institution (Willis, 1983), and considers that major post-war educational reforms in the industrial nations have failed to achieve their stated objectives of bringing about widespread social and economic change.

Several useful discussions of the new sociology of education or critical pedagogy literature have been published (Karabel & Halsey, 1976; Bates, 1980). Consequently, there is no need to treat it exhaustively here. It is helpful, though, to treat in broad outline some of its major themes and limitations as a backdrop to the search for a more appropriate theoretical framework within which to analyse schooling in a plural Canada.

Three of the most important contributions to the new sociology of education literature over the last two decades are reproduction theory, correspondence theory and resistance theory. A fourth contribution, one that focuses in detail on culture and its relationship to the school, has also considerably enhanced our knowledge and understanding. Each of the four contributions to theory owes much to the other three. It is probably too early, however, to describe their precise connections and inter-relationships with any degree of confidence. Therefore, while bearing in mind their relational aspects, each of the four theories will be analysed and presented in order. Particular attention will be paid to those aspects which possess special relevance and potential for improving our understanding of the impact of race and ethnicity in education. The limitations of the theories in this connection will also be identified. A brief summary section designed to help the reader keep this discussion clearly in mind during the second part of the book closes the chapter.

Reproduction theory

The French sociologist Bourdieu (1966) had a critical impact on the early stages of development of the new sociology of education with his argument that schools do not promote equality, but function principally to reproduce and sanction ascribed inequalities. The differences in educational achievement usually attributed to native or inherited ability, he argued, are in fact to be explained by sociological factors. Two of the latter, cultural capital and family ethos, possess particular explanatory value in that they vary considerably depending upon social background, and result in the initial inequalities observable among children beginning school. Bourdieu understood differences in cultural capital to occur primarily in three areas: verbal facility, general cultural background, and knowledge of the school system. By family ethos, he meant the expectations of school success within the family which the children in turn internalize. Not only do cultural capital and family ethos vary by socio-economic background, but the school also endorses the values of those of higher socio-economic standing and thereby reinforces existing inequalities and the promise of differential school success. As children from working-class backgrounds do not possess either the cultural capital or the value expectations that permeate the school system, their chances of achieving success are considerably reduced.

This concept of cultural capital was further developed by Bernstein (1971), who argued that different types of social relations generate different linguistic codes. Relations that are based on a common cultural identity and shared assumptions and expectations reduce the need to verbalize intent. Meanings can be left implicit, permitting the use of a simplified vocabulary and syntax, and resulting in the development of a restricted code of speech. In other types of social relations, however, where common culture, assumptions and expectations are lacking, intent cannot be taken for granted. In these situations, meanings have to be made explicit and expanded upon, giving rise to an elaborated speech code.

The most important influence on the formation of these two types of linguistic code, according to Bernstein, is social class. Elaborated speech codes he associated with the middle class, and restricted speech codes with the working class. The school adopts an elaborated speech code to which middle-class children have already been introduced by their families before entering school, but this was not so with children of the working class. Furthermore, despite similar intellectual potential, children who have access to different speech codes adopt different intellectual orientations which leads to differences in educational outcomes. As the social class structure regulates the message systems or knowledge codes of the school, working-class children experience discontinuity between their cultural capital and that endorsed by the school system. As a result, schools serve to help reproduce social class differences.

Advocates of reproduction theory reject any notion of the educational system as a closed and neutral system in which all children receive equal treatment and exposure to the same formal culture irrespective of background. On the contrary, they view education as a permeable system, one deeply affected by the differences in socio-economic standing and resources that children bring to the school. Thus to treat students as though they are equal, when in reality they are not, only permits and encourages the impact of the differences in the cultural capital they possess. Consequently, school success, which liberal-democratic theory views as the outcome of objective and open competition, is in effect the result of an unequal contest and is better explained by the school's acceptance, distribution and legitimation of a socially-determined cultural capital. To think otherwise, to endow the formal educational system with the appearance of equality, and to conceive of the cultural capital of the school in universal terms, only results in the reproduction of inequality.

Correspondence theory

The concept of reproduction is also present in the work of Bowles & Gintis (1976), whose names are most closely associated with the correspondence theory of education. These two scholars took the position that the school system in a capitalist society performs two major functions. It reproduces the necessary workforce for the operation of the capitalist system; and it provides the necessary ideology by which social class relations, which correspond closely to those of the workplace, are legitimized. That is, the school system allocates individuals to positions in the economic structure which are inherently unequal, given the hierarchical nature of the capitalist division of labour. In doing so, not only does it reproduce economic inequalities, it also distorts the personal growth and development of young people. Thus, although capitalism claims to embrace egalitarian ideals and emphasize individual growth and development, its educational system helps produce and reproduce a stratified society in which its social relations correspond highly with those of the economy.

This essentially Marxist analysis of schooling, while it undoubtedly exercised considerable influence among sociologists of education in North America and Europe, has also been the subject of intense critical discussion. Correspondence theory, its critics have argued, is far too deterministic and mechanistic. For example, the interlocking nature of social relations in the school and in the workplace is not as constant as correspondence theorists claim. Nor for that matter does the social organization of the classroom provide a mirror image of that found in economic life. Teachers and students are not merely passive agents, transmitters and consumers of the dominant culture. Knowledge is also mediated and produced in the school (Giroux, 1981). The economy does not reign supreme; classroom relations are not always static, and schools frequently serve as sites of opposition and resistance to the dominant culture (Willis, 1983). Conflicts occur along racial and ethnic as well as class lines and the conflicts that result possess their own dynamism (Breton *et al.*, 1979). Finally, consistently to view ethnicity in negative terms and automatically to consider it a barrier to progress hinders rather than advances analysis.

Resistance theory

Willis (1977) may be credited as the first writer in the sociology of education to develop a theory of schooling in which a central role is given to the idea of resistance. More recently, too, he has roundly criticized reproduction theorists for the absence in their analyses of schooling of any mention of the production and reproduction of culture by minority groups. The most fully developed criticism of social theorists who ignore the important role played by minority groups in resisting dominant group interpretations of culture and schooling, however, is to be found in the work of Giroux and especially the ideas he expressed in *Theory and Resistance in Education* (1983a).

Three elements of this work are worth commenting upon more fully. The first involves his penetrating criticism of traditional, neo-marxist, and reproductive theories of schooling. Traditional theory (both conservative and liberal) is roundly criticized both for its tendency to view schools merely as instructional sites, and for its seeming inability to see their importance as contested cultural and political sites. Marxist and neo-marxist theories of schooling are found wanting because they reduce resistance to a form of political style and fail to situate it within specifically political contexts and movements. Neo-marxists have very little to say on how students from different racial and cultural backgrounds resist varying types of control and domination in schools. Reproduction theorists, on the other hand, are criticized for their virtual exclusion of theories of resistance in their analyses of schooling. They are also chastized for employing models of domination that are inherently static. Bourdieu, for instance, is cited for his failure to acknowledge the importance of resistance, incorporation and accommodation in his analysis of cultural production and reproduction.

A second element of Giroux's contribution in *Theory and Resistance in Education* (1983a) that is worth noting is his exploration of the potential of resistance for initiating change. He begins his exploration by reviewing recent studies that have taken conflict and resistance as the starting points of their analyses and 'have sought to redefine the importance of power, ideology and culture as central constructs for understanding the complex relations between schooling and the dominant society' (1983: 98). They are valuable, he argues, because in order to lay bare the dynamics of resistance and accommodation, they integrate social theory with the findings of detailed ethnographic research. They also perform an important service by calling for more political analyses of schooling that embrace both theory and practice.

The third important element of Giroux's work on resistance theory is that, although he recognizes the significance of studies of power, ideology and culture, he is also aware of their limitations. Foremost among these in the present context is that they have failed to take factors of race and ethnicity sufficiently into account. Second, they have mistakenly elevated virtually every instance of oppositional behaviour to the level of organized resistance. Third, they have tended to romanticize all modes of resistance — even when they have contained reactionary views, for example, about women.

What then does Giroux suggest be done? Among other things, he calls for the development of a theory of resistance that clarifies the theoretical basis of schooling from the point of view of all of the actors involved. Such a theory would point to a new framework 'for examining schools as social sites, particularly the experience of subordinate groups' (1983a: 107). This would include examination of concepts such as hegemony, and questions such as whose culture is represented in the school curriculum and whose culture is excluded. Studies of the school from the viewpoint of racial and ethnic minorities would be stressed. Resistance is an active process involving interactions between lived experiences and the institutions and structures that attempt to shape them. It is a political act that involves actors, processes and structures internal and external to the educational system. In brief, Giroux directs attention to the ways in which minority individuals, and more importantly groups, 'can find a voice and maintain and extend the positive dimensions of their own cultures and histories' (1983a: 111).

The theory of culture

The fourth and final contribution of critical theorists to the new sociology of education literature involves the reappraisal of the theory of culture and its relationship to the school. Sociological definitions of culture generally find their basis in one or the other of two ideological traditions: liberal-democratic or Marxist. The former assumes that the individual, and individual expression, is the key element in the production of culture; the latter emphasizes the importance of the economic structure in its formation. Both traditions consider culture to be a central concept in any comprehensive theory of society, and both consider that public institutions play a central role in the production and reproduction of culture. Both accord it a significant place in their analyses of schooling, which of course are deeply affected by the assumptions that underly the two broad ideological traditions.

Culture has also been defined in a variety of ways in the social sciences. Many definitions, such as the following two, are general, all-embracing and open-ended.

> Culture consists of patterns, explicit and implicit, of and for behaviour acquired and transmitted by symbols, constituting the distinctive achievements of human groups including their embodiment in artifacts; the essential core of culture consists of traditional ideas and especially their attached values (*A Dictionary of the Social Sciences*, 1964).

The second definition reflects its anthropological antecedents and it too focuses attention on the group. Culture is defined as:

> the way of life of a social group; the group's man-made environment including all the material and non-material products of group life that are transmitted from one generation to the next; that whole complex which includes knowledge, belief, art, morals, customs and other capabilities and habits acquired by man as a member of society. (*A Modern Dictionary of Sociology*, 1981)

Both definitions stress the transmission of culture and give the impression that culture is relatively stable and unchanging. Implicitly both convey notions of cultural maintenance and reproduction.

Such relatively unproblematic definitions of culture have recently come under considerable criticism, however. The necessity of re-thinking the links between economic and political power and culture — especially the power of dominant groups to exercise control over cultural institutions like the school — have been stressed (Bourdieu & Passeron, 1977). Williams (1981) has called for the development of a political economy of culture that is distinct from that of cultural sociology. Willis (1983) has asserted that power and the structure of power is not an inert possession but a contested set of relations between groups. And Giroux (1981) has emphasized the need to politicize the concept of both culture and schooling.

Giroux (1983b) in his more recent analysis of the theory of culture has also provided a valuable discussion of the disagreements that nevertheless continue. Current disputes, for example, tend to centre around the views expressed by the 'culturalist' and the 'structuralist' schools of thought. The 'culturalist' perspective opposes all forms of reductionism and sees culture as a set of ideas and practices within which specific ways of life are integrated. Analyses of culture employing this perspective involve the study of relationships and are necessarily grounded in the activities of everyday life. Thus, for example, the 'culturalist' approach not only takes into account how dominant groups produce and reproduce culture, it also examines the same processes within subordinate groups, and pays attention to the relations between dominant and subordinate groups. In addition, it emphasizes the importance of setting, historical context, of human agency, struggle and conflict. The 'structuralist' perspective, on the other hand, emphasizes the primary importance of economic and political structures in producing and reproducing specific cultures. It considers the regulatory and mediating role of the state to be crucial to these processes, and class and class conflict as central and informing ideas. It views ideologies as fundamental sources of cohesion as well as conflict, and stresses the fact that they are deeply embedded in such social organizations as the school. Like the 'culturalist' perspective, it recognizes the role of competition and struggle in the formation of culture.

Along with the criticisms of definitions and interpretations of culture noted above, however, both perspectives offer insights into the relationship between culture, schooling and socio-political-economic systems. They note the supportive and oppositional elements that exist in a culture at one and the same time. They underline the fact that majority–minority relations are a dynamic not a static process, and that the exercise of power by the dominant group is continually being contested at the level of the school. Most importantly, they also permit for possibilities of change and transformation.

More specifically, current analyses of theories of culture have given rise to the identification, definition and application of a group of five related concepts that possess considerable analytical potential. Located mainly in, and drawing largely upon, power-conflict perspectives of group relations, these concepts nevertheless recognize the value of some forms of structural analysis. They may well offer, therefore, a most valuable framework for the analysis of schooling in a plural society.

Cultural hegemony

The first of the five concepts is that of cultural hegemony. Its assertion in the field of public education has been discussed by a number of critical social theorists, prominent among whom are Bourdieu & Passeron (1977). These authors defined cultural hegemony as the imposition by the dominant group of a specific cultural design based on its possession of power, whereby the group's culture was reproduced and distributed through a variety of institutions including the school. Giroux, (1981: 23) defined cultural hegemony as

> the successful attempt of a dominant class to utilize its control over the resources of the state and civil society, particularly through the use of the mass media and the educational system, to establish its view of the world as all inclusive and universal.

All three scholars, but particularly Giroux, believe that cultural hegemony is neither fixed nor unchanging. Rather, dominant groups need continually to renew their hegemony, authority and control. They do so, moreover, in the face of efforts by subordinate groups (including racial and cultural groups) to resist these forms of domination.

Cultural reproduction

The second concept, cultural reproduction, refers to the efforts by dominant and subordinate groups alike to transmit their knowledge, values, belief systems and behavioural norms from one generation to the next. The process is dynamic and is intimately connected to the process of social reproduction in which the social, economic and political characteristics of a group are reproduced. Not surprisingly, both are inseparably related to the reproduction of relations between dominant and subordinate racial and ethnic groups. These relations are the result of direct and indirect applications of power by the dominant group. Thus, what we often refer to as 'mainstream' culture is largely determined by these relations. That is, it is essentially compatible with and synonymous to the cultural tradition of the dominant group. It is, moreover, the outcome of desired and deliberate continuity of practice. Like tradition, 'mainstream' culture is reproduction in action.

Theories of reproduction as noted earlier are particularly valuable in the analysis of schooling. In particular, they provide insight into the processes whereby dominant group cultures reproduce themselves via large-scale modern institutional structures like the public education system (Williams, 1981). They offer an alternative perspective to the one that uncritically views schooling as automatically serving to promote the twin goals of equality of opportunity and social mobility. For while success in school has undoubtedly improved the life chances of many individuals, the evidence also indicates that schools have been less than successful with certain racial and ethnic groups. Why this is so may well be explained by the fact that it is the dominant group's cultural and linguistic traditions that are being reproduced in the schools and certain groups experience more difficulty than others in responding to these.

Cultural capital

The third concept, cultural capital, is perhaps best understood by way of analogy to those of human and physical capital. By viewing culture as a valuable resource, the control over form and content of which is contested, we can better understand the conflicts over schooling that are particularly acute in multiracial, multicultural societies. In such societies, of which Canada of course is one, the question of which specific knowledge, belief systems, values and patterns of behaviour are to be selected for transmission is problematic. It is not only a question of what culture and what heritage is to be reproduced (Hodgetts, 1968), but whose culture and whose heritage. Attempts to answer these questions, as we shall see, have long exercised the minds of educational policy-makers and developers of school curricula.

That certain types of values, knowledge and skill are more highly rated than others in public school systems is not in doubt. Why this is so, why such hierarchies exist, and the assumptions and criteria on which they rest, are much less clear. The concept of cultural capital, however, when linked to the concepts of cultural hegemony and cultural reproduction, suggests that the processes of selection and hierarchical ordering which take place are largely determined by the exercise of power by the dominant cultural group in order that the curriculum might reflect the group's preferred content, values and traditions. Language is a very clear case in point. With very few exceptions, the language of instruction is the language of the dominant or majority group. Schools, therefore, reinforce the role of language in mediating relationships between dominant and subordinate groups, and help produce, reproduce and legitimate differential relations among majority and minority, racial and ethno-cultural groups.

Cultural legitimation

The fourth concept, cultural legitimation, suggests that claims of legitimacy for school curricula and practices are largely derived from the relative amount of authority and power possessed by the dominant cultural group (Schermerhorn, 1970). For schools and school curricula not only transmit and distribute the cultural capital of the dominant group, they also legitimize it by conferring on it qualities of objectivity, neutrality, and even universality. At the same time, the cultural capital of subordinate groups, especially their languages, is marginalized and frequently excluded altogether. The implications of these processes in a plural society can readily by appreciated, for questions of societal integration are intimately related to questions of legitimacy, which must be achieved and reworked as conditions and relations undergo change. Legitimacy cannot be taken for granted, as its interpretation, and especially the arbitrary imposition of knowledge and culture, is frequently resisted by minority groups.

Cultural resistance

This brings us to our fifth concept: cultural resistance. Regrettably, sociologists and political scientists have paid scant attention to the efforts of subordinate racial and ethno-cultural groups to resist the marginalization and replacement of their cultures and languages. Even when they have focused on the dysfunctional aspects of the educational system, they have generally neglected to explain why the system seems to work to the advantage of certain groups and not others. Their explanations have not been pursued 'in terms of the groups that make up society, the source of their power, and the contradictions that these involve ... they do not conceive of resistance on the part of those who are disadvantaged by the operation of the system' (Murphy, 1979: 50). Analyses of educational disadvantage in fact have usually been interpreted in terms of social class. Race, ethnicity and gender have received but minor attention (Barton & Walker, 1983).

It is for these reasons that the theories of resistance advanced by Giroux (1981, 1983) are particularly relevant. Giroux, it will be recalled, criticized the seeming inability of functionalist theories of education to view schools as other than instructional sites. Power-conflict theorists were found wanting in that although they seek 'to redefine the importance of power, ideology and culture as central constructs for understanding the complex relations between schooling and the dominant society', and although they recognize the need for more political analyses of schooling, they nevertheless uncritically elevate all forms of opposition to the level of organized resistance (1983a: 98). Reproduction theorists, much of whose work Giroux values, are criticized for their failure to treat the processes of minority group cultural production and reproduction. As well, radical theorists are chastized for their tendency to interpret the process of domination and its effects in largely static and unchanging terms.

On the other hand, Giroux declares that it is patently obvious that schools are contested cultural and political sites. For him culture is to be defined as "lived antagonistic relations" situated within a complex of socio-political institutions and social forms that limit as well as enable human action. Culture is the instance of mediation between a society and its institutions (such as schools) and the experiences of those (such as teachers and students) who are in the institution daily (1981: 18, 19). The schools are contested political sites because the creation of public educational policy and its implementation is a political act that is frequently the subject of resistance and challenge. Resistance, moreover, must be a conscious and deliberate act aimed at achieving change and carrying within it the possibilities of transformation.

Conclusion

Probably the most important contribution of theorists in the new sociology of education, although admittedly not an entirely novel one, is their insistence that educational systems are not as autonomous as many previous commentators would have had us believe. Schools, they argue, should be seen for what they are: part of a much larger, interlocking pattern of institutions, structures and processes — political, economic, social and cultural. This pattern, moreover, exerts considerable influence and control over the role and practice of schooling, an idea which has been expressed particularly well by Raymond Williams:

> the pattern of meanings and values through which people conduct their whole lives can be seen for a time as autonomous, and as evolving within its own terms, but this is quite unreal, ultimately to separate this pattern from a precise political and economic system which can extend its influence into the most unexpected regions of feeling and behaviour. The common prescription of education, as the key to change, ignores the fact that the form and content of education are affected, and in some cases determined, by the actual systems of (political) decisions and (economic) maintenance (cited in Apple, 1979: 27, 28).

Any analysis of education that ignores the fact that the form and content of education are affected, in some cases determined, by the political and economic decision-making systems, is likely therefore to be off-target.

Another important contribution of the theorists is their emphasis on the fact that the school's relationship to the broader political and economic system is informed by a complex set of differential power relations. The importance of this insight for the study of schooling in a plural society should not be overlooked. Clearly, dominant groups exercise considerable control over the public schools, their governance, administration and curricula. The latter are the result of a series of conscious selections made by the dominant group from a larger cultural tradition in which the knowledge, skills and values it considers important are prominently featured. The hierarchical structure and organization of the curriculum reflects these judgements. Different allocations of time, resources and status accorded various subjects of study confirm them. Alternative forms, especially those advanced by subordinate ethnic groups, are treated as supplementary activities or excluded altogether. Why this is so is rarely made explicit, however. Assumptions remain tacit, as do epistemological commitments, and are generally passive, consensus-oriented, and un-critically supportive of existing economic, political, ideological and intellectual frameworks (Pratt, 1975).

A third and highly significant contribution is that subordinate groups frequently resist the marginalization of their cultures, histories and languages. Thus resistance, it has been pointed out, is frequently expressed via the highly visible, tax-supported public school system. The school and the school curriculum often serve as arenas of contestation and struggle. Such resistance also serves the purpose of affirming a subordinate group's value system and sense of identity, thereby contributing to its long-term survival.

Finally, the concepts we have examined in this chapter are dynamic concepts subject to varying degrees of interpretation and change. To fully appreciate their significance, therefore, recognition must be accorded to the importance of context and setting. There must be a firm grounding in concrete settings, and account must be taken of regional, local and group differences. It is appropriate, then, at this point, to turn from a consideration of theory to an analysis of culture, conflict and schooling in Canada.

PART II:
The Canadian context

Three broad and competing sets of principles and assumptions about what constitutes or should constitute the authentic nature of Canadian society and culture can be identified. These are referred to in a variety of ways in the literature but may usefully be clustered under the respective headings of monoculturalism, biculturalism and multiculturalism. Monoculturalism stresses the unity and oneness of Canadian society and culture; biculturalism is rooted firmly in the principle of English–French duality; and multiculturalism is linked to broader notions of pluralism.

Each of the three concepts possesses adherents and an ideology or mutually supportive matrix of ideas and images. Each sponsors and shapes public policy stances on issues relating to culture. Each, for example, is associated with one or other of three positions on language — unilingualism, bilingualism and multilingualism. And each has exerted considerable influence over the goals, content and governance of education.

The presence of three competing versions of Canada and Canadian culture has inevitably resulted in tensions, struggles and conflicts. Over time, and in different settings and locales, racial tensions, religious struggles, linguistic strife and conflicts over schooling have formed significant leitmotifs in Canadian history. The images and ideologies associated with conformist, dualistic and pluralistic concepts of Canada have varied as a result. Each has affected the other and has been affected in turn.

Culture, intergroup relations and schooling are dynamic processes, frequently contested and continuously being produced, reproduced and resisted. It is to an examination of these processes in the Canadian context that we now turn. Chapter 4, 'Culture, Conflict and Schooling', deals with the recurring conflicts over culture that have so often erupted in the schools. A brief historical background section serves as an introduction to the general theme and is followed by specific analyses of three major sub-themes: assimilation, bilingualism and biculturalism, and multi-culturalism within a bilingual framework. Criticisms of the latter policy, an attenuated form of pluralism, are reviewed, along with their implications for present and future developments.

Chapter 5, 'Major Issues', presents an up-to-date look at five interrelated issues around which controversies currently swirl: governance of education, official language minority educational rights, and schooling in non-official languages. The section on educational governance examines the struggle of the aboriginal peoples to obtain authority and control over the schools their children attend. Official language educational rights are examined in the context of court judgements dealing with the interpretations of these rights in *The Canadian Charter of Rights and Freedoms* (1982). The issue of schooling in the non-official languages is examined from the perspective of recent efforts by non-official language groups to have their languages find a legitimate and valid place in the public school systems. Chapter 6 provides a brief summary and perspective of schooling in a modern plural society.

4 Culture, conflict and schooling

Introduction

Efforts to ensure the dominance of one culture over another in Canada have been a recurring source of conflict since the arrival of the Europeans in sizeable numbers in the seventeenth century. The Europeans, believing themselves and their societal forms, race and cultures to be far superior to those of the various aboriginal peoples, made systematic efforts to denigrate and oppress aboriginal cultures, values and languages. Over time the application of this sense of cultural superiority included the encroachment on Indian ancestral lands, their forcible expropriation and the segregation of Indians on reserves. As settlement expanded, the aboriginal peoples were stripped of military power, their lands absorbed, their economies further disrupted and their life-styles devalued. Dominant group interests and implicit and explicit policies of segregation and assimilation were pursued. Where schooling was concerned, cultural, religious and linguistic replacement were major objectives, and assimilation to one or other of the two dominant cultures a major goal. Yet despite this history of racism, exploitation and oppression, the efforts of the aboriginal peoples to resist assimilation have proved remarkably durable.

Conflict also occurred among the citizens of the two major European colonizing powers: France and England. Both groups struggled to establish the primacy of their culture, language, laws and institutions and consequently relations between French- and English-Canadians came to play a central, some would argue *the* central, role in Canadian economic, political and social affairs. In the mid-eighteenth century, for example, following their refusal to swear allegiance to the British Crown the Francophone Acadians were deported from Nova Scotia and New Brunswick.

Rebellions in Lower Canada (Quebec) and Upper Canada (Ontario) in support of responsible self-government in both provinces occurred but were quickly suppressed (1837–38). Lord Durham, in his report of 1839, proposed to the British Crown that the problems of French–English relations be resolved by the union of Upper and Lower Canada, a union in which the Francophones would become a minority. His advice was heeded and a year later *The Act of Union* (1840) established the Province of Canada. An equal number of members were elected to its Assembly from Upper and Lower Canada, but its official language was English — this at a time when the Francophone population of Lower Canada numbered 650,000 and the Anglophone population of Upper Canada 450,000. Not until 1864, in fact, was legislation passed stipulating that both English and French could be used in the Assembly of the Province of Canada as well as in the legislature of Lower Canada (Bourhis, 1984).

Passage of the historic *British North America Act* (1867) provides further evidence (if any is needed) that the issue of culture in Canada is pre-eminently a political issue. This Act, which formed the centrepiece of the Canadian Constitution until very recently, declared the Dominion of Canada to be composed of four provinces: Ontario, Quebec, Nova Scotia and New Brunswick. It established a federal form of government, the major rationale for which was the recognition of diversity, the need to accommodate minority concerns, and the desire for territorial integration (Watts, 1970). In doing so, it embraced 'the idea that institutions and social forces affect each other, (that) neither is wholly dependent as an effect of the other, and that modern society is both dynamic and diversified' (Black, 1975: 9). A concrete example of the motivations that spurred these Fathers of Confederation and one that underlines the potential for religious and cultural conflict that existed, was their decision to move education 'out of the national political system and into the sub-systems of the provinces where the differences flourished' (Mallory, 1976: 2). A conscious effort was thus made to ensure 'that all Canadians could retain their historic cultural identities while at the same time sharing economically, militarily and in international affairs and the benefits of a larger nation' (Cook, 1977: 15).

It was, however, at least from the point of view of religious and cultural minorities, a largely unsuccessful effort. For example, while passage of a Quebec law in 1869 ensured Anglophone Protestants control over their own school system, legislation in New Brunswick in 1871 restricted funding to non-confessional schools. As result Francophone Catholics had to finance their own schools, or failing that, to attend those of the Anglophone majority. A second province, Manitoba (which in 1870 had declared French and English as official languages and guaranteed the existence of both Catholic and Protestant schools), abolished confessional schools in 1890, and banned the use of the French language in the legislature and judicial systems. Henceforth, laws were to be passed and published in English only. In Ontario, where in 1912 Francophones made up 20% of the population, Regulation 17 banned the teaching of French in all public schools. Four years later, a similar ban was imposed in Manitoba. Further west in Saskatchewan the teaching of French was abolished in Anglophone school boards in 1929. In the same province, in 1942–46, the government re-drew the boundaries of its school districts, and as a consequence Francophones lost control of their educational system.

Conflicts over the relationship between culture and schooling also became more complex with the arrival of growing numbers of immigrants of different racial and ethnocultural backgrounds. Beginning in the mid-nineteenth century, and coinciding to a large extent with the settlement of the prairies, a massive wave of immigration occurred. Attracted by Canada's expansionary promises and the need for labour, the new immigrants helped settle the territories which were to become Manitoba, Alberta and Saskatchewan. As early as 1921, groups of non-Anglophones and non-Francophones background (more recently referred to as Allophones) formed between 30 and 40% of the prairie population. Fifty years later, in 1971, they formed 25.3% of the total population.

Jaenen (1972) has reminded us that the cultures, religions and languages of Allophone groups gave rise to a number of controversies over schooling in the 'settlement' period 1867–1920. He draws our attention, for example, to a neglected area of Canada's educational history in his discussion of the minority rights of Mennonites, Mormons, Hutterites, Doukhobors and Ukrainians (or 'Ruthenians'). Initially, it seems, some degree of flexibility existed with regard to schooling. On arrival in Manitoba, for example, the Mennonites discovered that the Protestant school system met their religious needs while the legal vacuum with respect to languages of instruction enabled them to teach in German. The Ukrainians, who according to Jaenen appear to have expected little or no pressure for linguistic assimilation on arriving in Canada, were among the largest groups in Manitoba shortly after the provisions for bilingual schooling were enacted in 1897. In 1905, a Ruthenian Training School was opened in Winnipeg and later moved to Brandon to train Ukrainian-English bilingual teachers. By 1915, a quarter of the province's schools, comprising one-sixteenth of the total enrolment, were bilingual schools.

Initial recognition of cultural diversity in education can also be noted in the Northwest Territories. Here, in 1901, the Territorial Assembly permitted any language to be taught in the schools for one hour each day on such days as the local school board determined. The hope was that the policy would encourage groups to establish schools. As a practice, it continued after 1905 when the provinces of Saskatchewan and Alberta were formed (McLeod, 1980). And although neither province had statutory provisions for bilingual schooling, the Saskatchewan government opened a Training School for Teachers for Foreign-Speaking Communities in Regina in 1909.

Soon, however, the degrees of freedom permitted to Allophone groups in the area of schooling were reduced and then all but abolished. The onset of World War I and the feelings it fueled only hastened the process and inscribed it with an intensity amounting to hysteria (Jaenen, 1972). In Manitoba, and to a very large extent in Saskatchewan, all provisions for teaching in languages other than English were removed (McLeod, 1980). The remaining Mennonite private schools were abolished and parents jailed for refusing to comply with compulsory school attendance laws. In 1919 the courts declared that the Lowe memorandum of 1873 was not binding on the Manitoba government in matters of education. Between 1922 and 1924 about 5,000 Mennonites left for Mexico and in 1926–27 another 1,700 left for Paraguay (Jaenen, 1972).

At least one historian of Canadian immigration (Palmer, 1984) has concluded that at best Anglo-Canadians were 'reluctant hosts' during the period 1867–1920 in which the prairies were settled. Proponents of Anglo-conformity considered new arrivals had an obligation to conform to existing values and institutions. Belief in God, King and country as well as 'progress' were the verities of the time, and the superiority of an imperialistic civilization was taken largely for granted. Indeed, during World War I, loyalty and cultural and linguistic uniformity were considered by many Anglophones to be synonymous. These values underwrote the then existing policies of immigration, and prevailing assumptions about the relative assimilability of different groups were transformed into a public debate as to whether certain groups should be allowed to enter the country. Asian immigrants — the Chinese, Japanese and East Indians — and black immigrants were considered least assimilable. Since this was the case, many intellectuals and politicians concluded, 'immigrants who were culturally or racially in-ferior and incapable of being assimilated, either culturally or biologi-cally, would have to be excluded' (Palmer, 1984: 24).

Assimilation

The assimilationist ideology, which exercises considerable influence over perceptions of the role and function of public schooling in Canada, is one of the three sub-themes to be explored in this chapter on culture, conflict and schooling. Historically, as we shall see, it is an ideology that has possessed powerful appeal, and at one time or another has been invoked to justify the assimilation of the native peoples, Francophones and generation after generation of immigrants. The legacy of this appeal is still very much with us, as can be seen by contemporary attempts to promote Franco-conformity in Quebec as well as Anglo-conformity elsewhere.

This is not to suggest that the English speaking majority held common positions on public schooling. Some (Methodists, for example), believed that the state should accept the primary responsibility to educate children; others (Anglicans, in particular) felt quite comfortable with a denominational school system which the state helped to finance. Some opposed classes in French or German or other languages because they wanted a unilingual Canada. Others opposed them for the same reason they opposed classes in other subjects (such as ancient history or physical education) because they thought schools should concentrate on inculcating basic skills and information. In effect, then, the use of schools to assimilate minorities was of more importance to some members of the majority than to others. Similarly, resistance to assimilationist pressures among minority groups differed; rarely to date has their opposition coalesced to the point of cooperative action. Much more historical research, especially case-studies displaying a variety of theoretical and interpretive frameworks, is needed if we are to fully appreciate the importance of historical contest and human agency in the struggle of minorities to obtain public schooling appropriate to their needs and interests.

Acknowledging that interpretations of assimilationist ideology differ from period to period and place to place, these interpretations nevertheless possess three features in common: pressures towards assimilation usually originate with the dominant group or culture; subordinate groups and cultures traditionally resist such pressures by seeking to maintain their own institutions; and the outcomes of these pressures and resistances vary considerably depending upon the relative amounts of power and status the groups possess.

Valuable historical reviews of Canadian assimilation (Brown *et al.*,

1969; Jaenen, 1972; and Palmer, 1976) exist and it is not our intent to examine these in detail here. We have already noted, for example, the efforts of church and state to use the schools to systematically replace the cultures of the aboriginal peoples. Residential church schools in which it was forbidden for pupils to use their native languages were in the vanguard of these efforts, as were provincial education systems designed with the white majority firmly in mind. That they were unsuccessful for the most part in promoting student success in these unfamiliar and often irrelevant contexts has not deterred their supporters however. Tacit assimilationist assumptions still underly much of the educational policy governing the school experience of aboriginal children (*Indian Control of Indian Education*, 1972; Berger, 1977). This attitude continues despite passive resistance expressed by the extremely low retention rates for Indian children in public high schools, and despite the increasingly active and politicized resistance of indigenous peoples' organizations (see Chapter 5).

A second persistent application of assimilationist ideology is to be found in the area of education of Francophone minorities outside Quebec. As one of Canada's leading Anglophone historians has affirmed, the rejection of Lord Durham's recommendation that Francophone minorities be gradually assimilated into the English-speaking majority has frequently been overlooked in practice.

> In the 1870s in New Brunswick, Catholic school rights were modified in a manner that reduced French language education. In the 1890s in Manitoba, schools which Franco-Manitobans believed had been guaranteed by the Manitoba Act of 1870 were denied any further financial support, and French was abolished as an official language. In 1915 the same province withdrew what little "bilingual" teaching remained. The other prairie provinces imitated the Manitoba pattern. As for Ontario, where the largest numbers of French Canadians outside Quebec lived, Regulation 17, adopted in 1913, struck down the hopes of Franco-Ontarians that in numbers at least there might be safety. Even when that regulation was repealed in 1927, little change took place. No wonder then that many French Canadians outside Quebec and in Quebec itself, concluded that Henri Bourassa, the great newspaperman and politician, was right when he said that French Canadians, like the Canadian Indians, could only exercise their treaty rights when they remained on 'the reserve' in Quebec. (Cook, 1977: 15).

Similarly, until very recently in Western Canada, the view prevailed that

Canada was essentially an English country, and as far as the West was concerned, there was no place for the perpetuation of any form of duality in a region composed of many peoples of various backgrounds. What was required was the integration, if not the total assimilation, of incoming groups into what could only be an English-speaking community. (Painchaud, 1976)

Assimilationist ideology was applied in its most explicit and energetic form to immigrants of non-French and non-British background. All the major books on immigration published prior to 1920, and written by progressives and reactionaries alike, (including J. S. Wordsworth's *Strangers Within Our Gates*; Ralph Connor's *The Foreigner*; Alfred Fitzpatrick's *Handbook for New Canadians*; C. A. Magrath's *Canada's Growth and Some Problems Affecting It*; C. B. Sisson's *Bilingual Schools in Canada*; and W. G. Smith's *A Study in Canadian Immigration*) were based on assumptions of Anglo-conformity.

The answer to all the problems of social diversity which the immigrants posed was assimilation. The difficulty however with achieving this goal of assimilation was not only the large numbers of immigrants, or the fact that not all (or even a majority) of them wanted to be assimilated. One of the major factors preventing assimilation was discrimination by the Anglo-Canadian majority. (Palmer, 1984: 27)

Extensive patterns of social, economic and political discrimination developed and were reflected in educational structures and institutions.

In the years immediately following World War I and coincident with a second main wave of immigration, a second ideology of assimilation appeared. This was the 'melting pot' ideology which drew heavily on ideas developed in the United States of America. It arose in part as a means of defending immigrants against nativist attacks, and proposed a biological merging and blending of cultures into a new Canadian identity. Assimilation, its supporters argued, was occurring, but to a new Canadian type. Immigrants, moreover, could and would make some valuable cultural contributions in the process. Thus although advocates of both Anglo-conformity and the melting pot theory believed that uniformity was ultimately necessary for unity, they disagreed as to its basis. The former thought it rested on an explicit commitment to British institutions and values; the latter saw merit in gradualism and the possibilities of enrichment that a merging of nationalities and cultures would bring.

During the 1930s, and despite what he referred to as the 'vicious circle of discrimination', Palmer (1976) observed the arrival on the Canadian scene of the first major advocates of cultural pluralism. Influenced by a liberalism which rejected the assumptions of Anglophone superiority, writers like John Murray Gibbon (1938) in *The Canadian Mosaic* and Watson Kirkconnell (1935) demonstrated a familiarity and sympathy with the cultural backgrounds of immigrants. Both believed ethnic diversity was not incompatible with national unity. Their concepts of pluralism, however, did not exclude notions of assimilation altogether. Gibbon saw individual assimilation occurring as a result of participation in common institutions, and Kirkconnell believed it necessary in the realm of political and economic values and institutions.

Even their limited interpretations of cultural pluralism, however, were shared by few of their contemporaries. The earlier ideology of assimilation to Anglo-conformist models and institutions, particularly in the field of education and schooling, prevailed. Far from adopting a positive stance towards differences in culture and language, public educational systems worked to eradicate them. Normative declarations of unity within diversity notwithstanding, assimilation was their major preoccupation, practice and goal. Not until well after World War II, and then as a result of determined resistance from Indian, Francophone and Allophone groups, did the assimilationist ideology become less explicit, and support for policies of Anglo-conformity gradually fall into disrepute.

Bilingualism and biculturalism

The conflict over efforts to establish the concept of Canada as a bilingual, bicultural nation is firmly rooted in deep differences of opinion over the nature and applicability of the historic principle of duality in Canadian life and institutions. Constitutional efforts to protect this duality in the century after Confederation, and especially its application in the schools, were doomed to failure. By the middle of the nineteenth century, French-speaking members of the population were already outnumbered, and successive waves of immigration only reinforced this fact. As the country expanded westwards, attempts to protect and expand the principle of dualism, by force of arms as well as political negotiation, also proved unsuccessful. As a result, a century after Confederation, Francophones formed a numerical minority in every province except Quebec. In the interim, despite vigorous resistance, the provision of French-language education had been seriously curtailed and eroded. Such resistance, however, helped keep alive the concept of Canada as a bilingual, bicultural nation. Nowhere was this more evident than in Quebec, where in the years after World War II the links between culture, conflict and schooling took on renewed significance and political force.

The rapid development of the Canadian economy following World War II resulted in equally rapid social and cultural change (Mann, 1970). In Quebec these changes were so extensive as to earn the title the 'Quiet Revolution'. As a consequence, and within a very short space of time, the majority Francophone population found itself immersed in a process of secular change that traditionally its clerical and social élite had resisted. All of its major institutions — economic, political, religious and educational — were transformed. Fundamental shifts occurred in individual and collective expectations, and in the aftermath of change, many Francophone Quebecers sought exclusive control over their language and culture.

The status of a group's language, especially its place in the economy and the school system, is a reflection of its standing and power in a society. In a newly-emerging Quebec, therefore, it is hardly surprising that the language of instruction in schools became a focus of political interest and conflict. French-Canadian nationalism, always a potent factor in the province, took on new forms of expression, and one of these was the development of a heightened self-consciousness and awareness of the links between culture and schooling. A *Royal Commission of Inquiry on Education* (known after its chairman, Alphonse-Marie Parent, as the *Parent Commission*) was established in 1961 and reported in 1966. One of its main recommendations was that the provincial government had a major responsibility to protect the French language, regulate its use, encourage its improvement, and ensure the fullest possible development of the culture it expressed. To achieve these goals, a fundamental re-ordering of attitudes — a social solidarity that superceded all other claims and loyalties — was not only recommended but essential. It was somewhat surprising, therefore, that the Commission, while recognizing the right of the provincial government to introduce enforcing legislation on the language of instruction, did not recommend that it do so. Instead, it called for closer ties between the Francophone and Anglophone educational systems, and observed that all would be well as soon as the province's French-language schools offered an education of unquestioned quality (Quebec, 1966).

Why the Commission assumed this position can perhaps best be explained by its assumption that the school was the key agency in

Quebec for the protection and transmission of French language and culture. That is, it viewed the work of the school in an economic and political vacuum (Mallea, 1977a). A similar assumption runs through the reports of *The Royal Commission on Bilingualism and Biculturalism* (hereafter referred to as the *B and B Commission*), which was established by the federal government in l963. Like the *Parent Commission*, this Commission assumed that the school was the 'basic agency for maintaining language and culture' (Canada, Book I, 1967: 125). And like its predecessor, it too tended to view schooling in rather apolitical terms. This was a surprising ommission, given that it was established to help resolve what the Commission itself saw as the country's greatest political crisis.

The *B and B Commission* came into being at the prompting of members of both Francophone and Anglophone élites concerned over the growing alienation of a revitalized and assertive Quebec. Here was a French-language community determined to set aside what it perceived to be its traditionally subordinate role in a federal Canadian state. If it could not do so, it was prepared to seriously examine alternative options including those of separation and independence. The Commission, whose mandate was to recommend measures to ensure that the Canadian Confederation might develop 'according to the principle of equality between its two founding peoples' (Canada, Book III, Part 2, 1969: 351), recognized these realities. It was also aware, as its title indicates, that in the minds of many Francophones issues of language and culture symbolized the larger inequalities of economic and political power.

Studies mounted by the Commission documented glaring inequalities between Anglophones and Francophones in all areas of Canadian life: political, economic, social and educational. Political imbalances between the two groups, especially at the federal level, were well known. Now the existence of marked economic differences in the world of work were identified and substantiated. Francophone incomes, for example, were found to be 'conspicuously lower in Canada as a whole, in the individual provinces, in specific cities, and in specific industries and occupations' (Canada, Book III, Part 4, 1969: 543). Similar disparities in terms of educational attainment were discovered between the two linguistic and cultural groups. According to the Commission, 'grave inequalities' existed in opportunities for French-speaking minorities (as compared to Anglophone minorities) to receive an education in their mother tongue (Canada, Book I, 1967: 121).

The Commission concluded that a major cause of these inequalities, which resulted in Francophones outside of Quebec losing their language, was the

> unwillingness of the English-speaking majority to recognize the right of French-speaking parents to educate their children in French. In Quebec, where the right to equal access to an education in either official language has been respected, even remote and numerically insignificant English-speaking communities have been provided with reasonable opportunities for schooling in English. In most of the other provinces, until very recently, such teaching in French as was permitted was intended simply as a means of transition to the English language. Parents who wanted their children educated in their language and their culture had to bear the costs of a private education while still having to contribute to the English-language public school system. (1967: 122)

This situation the Commissioners considered unacceptable. Equal partnership in a bilingual Canada implied the fullest development of both languages compatible with regional circumstances. For the Commissioners, this meant that it must be accepted as normal that children of Francophone as well as Anglophone groups should have access to schools in which their own language was the language of instruction (1967: 123). In addition, they took the view that as schools were the formal means by which a society transmitted its knowledge, skills, languages and culture from one generation to the next, Canada's public school systems were primarily concerned with the transmission of knowledge that is essential to all citizens, including knowledge about Canadian institutions, the traditions and circumstances that have shaped them, and the two official languages. Since those of British and French ethnic origin were the main groups in Canada, it was 'appropriate that the British and French cultures (should) dominate in the public school systems' (Canada, Book IV, 1970: 137).

Before the federally-appointed *B and B Commission* could complete and publish all of its reports, a *Commission of Inquiry on the Position of the French Language and/or Language Rights in Quebec* (hereafter referred to as the *Gendron Commission*) was appointed by the Quebec government (1968). One of the factors which prompted its establishment was the existence of a serious conflict over schooling that became widely known in Quebec as *L'Affaire Saint-Leonard*. In November 1967, the Saint-Leonard School Commission, located in the north-east section of

Montreal, proposed the phasing out of a bilingual French-English program in schools enrolling large numbers of children of Italian immigrants, and replacing it with a unilingual French program. Many parents were fiercely opposed to the proposal and resisted its introduction. In June 1968, following hotly contested school elections, control of the School Commission passed into the hands of those committed to the introduction of the unilingual French program. Shortly thereafter they passed a resolution phasing out the bilingual French–English program. This action was viewed by immigrant and English-speaking members of the community as explicit discrimination against themselves and their children. Consequently, they moved quickly and angrily to organize and launch a vigorous counter-attack. The conflict soon escalated, spilling over its local boundaries and attracting considerable attention throughout the province. Street demonstrations ended in violence. The Quebec government was reluctantly drawn into the dispute and promised to introduce legislation to resolve it.

In December 1968, the Union Nationale government of Premier Bertrand introduced Bill 85 designed to ameliorate the situation. This it failed to do. Francophone reaction to the Bill was uniformly negative. Various pressure groups went on the offensive, and conflict over the Bill's provisions heightened. Francophone nationalists objected strenuously to the inclusion of the principle of parental choice of the language of instruction; Anglophones, on the other hand, expressed concern over the powers of implementation contained in the Bill. Such were the passions aroused that no compromise agreements could be reached. And in March 1969, the Premier withdrew the Bill, noting that it was 'un bebe que personne ne veut'. The conflict over language of instruction did not abate, however. In October 1969, a second piece of legislation, Bill 63, *An Act to Promote the French Language*, was introduced. It also included the option for parents to select either French or English as the language of instruction for their children's education. And once again, it was attacked by Francophone nationalists who argued that this provision placed the survival of the French language, and by extension French-Canadian culture, in jeopardy. Instead of providing parental freedom of choice, declared René Lévesque, access to English as the language of instruction should be restricted to Anglophones. The children of immigrants should be required to attend school in French.

Despite the vocal opposition of many Francophones, Bill 63 was passed. Parents now enjoyed freedom of choice over the language of instruction for their children. The issue was far from being resolved, however. During the years that Bill 63 remained in place, its provisions were a continual source of unrest. Consequently in May 1974, and subsequent to the receipt and study of the report of the *Gendron Commission*, the majority Liberal government of the day introduced new legislation aimed at defusing the conflict. Bill 22, titled the *Official Language Act*, declared French to be the sole official language of Quebec. In addition, it required school boards to administer language tests to the children of immigrants to determine whether they were to be placed in English-language or French-language schools. The proposed legislation provoked an immediate and furious response from all sides. It did so, according to one close observer, because it fell between two poles of public opinion representing two conflicting principles.

> The Anglophones and non-Francophone immigrants were committed for the most part to the principle of bilingualism and to the absolute right of parents to choose the language of instruction of their children. The Francophones were devoted to what they regarded as their collective right to exist as a nation and to making French at least the priority language and therefore primary vehicle of integration of immigrants. (Stein, 1977: 253)

Bill 22 pleased no one. Francophone unilingualists believed it did not go far enough in promoting French minority rights; Anglophones believed the rights they had gained under Bill 63 had been lost; and Allophones complained bitterly of discrimination. Despite, or perhaps because of, the entrenched resistance to its provisions, the Liberal government invoked closure and passed the Bill in July 1974. A response was not long in coming. An incensed Anglophone minority waged a full-blown media campaign aimed at having the Act repealed. Its members launched three court actions, two of which centred on the educational provisions of the new Act. But by far the most successful challenge came from the newly formed Parti-Québecois. With René Lévesque at its head, this part made repeal of Bill 22 one of the chief planks in its electoral platform, and following its stunning victory at the polls on 15th November, 1976, the party prepared to make good on its promise. Indeed, the new session of the National Assembly had hardly begun when the Parti-Québecois introduced a White Paper on the *Charter of the French Language*. The Charter signalled the party's intentions in clear and unambiguous fashion. In introducing it, the Minister of State for Cultural Development declared that the bill on the French language was to be given top priority. By giving it the status of a charter, the government sought to emphasize the special importance attached to it.

Bill 101, the *Charter of the French Language*, which became law on 26th August, 1977, recognized five fundamental language rights. The fifth of these established the right of every person eligible for instruction in Quebec to receive that instruction in French. In addition, an entire chapter of the law (Chapter VIII), consisting of sixteen clauses, was devoted to provisions concerning the language of instruction in schools. The first of these, Clause 72, required that instruction in kindergarten classes and in elementary and secondary schools be in French. Certain specified exceptions to the clause were also spelled out. The most important exception was contained in Section 72. It dealt with access to schools in which English is the language of instructions and read:

> In degradation of section 72, the following children at the request of the father and mother, may receive instruction in English:
>
> 1. a child whose father or mother received his or her elementary instruction in English, in Quebec;
> 2. a child whose father or mother, domiciled in Quebec on the date of coming into force of this act, received his or her elementary instruction in English outside Quebec;
> 3. a child who, in his last year of school in Quebec, before the coming into force of this act, was lawfully receiving his instruction in English, in a public kindergarten class or in an elementary or secondary school;
> 4. the younger brothers and sisters of a child described in paragraph (c).

The language of instruction provisions contained in Chapter VIII had three major purposes. They were drawn up in such a manner as to ensure that the school system reinforce French as the primary language of use in the province; they placed restrictions on the admission of children to English-language schools in order to prevent the future growth of these schools; and they required the children of immigrants to enrol in French language schools, thereby facilitating their eventual integration into the province's Francophone community.

Francophone reaction to Bill 101 was generally that of considerable gratification, and contrasted dramatically with that of an apprehensive Anglophone minority. The latter's reaction was immediate, vocal and impassioned. Media campaigns were launched accompanied by intense political lobbying at both the provincial and federal levels. Protests, moreover, centred on the Bill's minority language education provisions and their impact. Resistance in particular formed around the following four concerns:

1. The retroactive effects of clause 73, which declared inadmissible to English language education all French Quebecers and all

non-Francophones, residing in Quebec before August 1977, who for a variety of reasons could not conform to one or other of the provisions contained in the clause.

2. The restrictions placed on the mobility of Canadian citizens in other provinces whose children, on taking up permanent residence in Quebec, would be obliged to undertake their schooling in French.

3. That parents' secondary education in English is excluded as a criterion of eligibility for children to enter English language schools.

4. The effects of the legislation on the English language school boards in the province — especially its impact on enrolments and future growth.

(Mallea, 1984).

The first three of these primarily affect the lives of individuals, while the fourth has significant consequences at the system level. Each figured prominently in the legal challenges to the Bill that were commenced by the Anglophone and Allophone communities of Montreal (see Chapter 5).

Multiculturalism

The third concept of Canadian culture and society to attract widespread support is that based on one or other interpretations of cultural pluralism or multiculturalism. Many Allophones, of course, opposed both assimilationist ideologies (Franco- as well as Anglo-conformist) and biculturalism, and in the post-World War II period pluralist ideas were increasingly accepted.

By 1961, 26% of the Canadian population was of other than British or French ethnic origin; over 200 newspapers were being published in languages other than French and English; there were fairly well-defined Italian, Jewish, Slavic and Chinese neighbourhoods in large Canadian cities, and there were visible rural concentrations of Ukrainians, Doukhobors, Hutterites and Mennonites scattered across the western provinces: thus, how was it possible for a royal commission to speak of Canada as a bicultural country? (Palmer, 1976: 36)

Were those of neither French nor English background to be considered second-class citizens? Were their cultures, belief systems, values and languages to be allowed to wither and die out? Did their organizations and their institutions have no contribution to make in a dynamic and evolving society?

The *Parent*, *Gendron* and *B and B Commissions* had all noted the increasingly culturally diverse nature of society but had accorded it a subordinate role in their analyses of culture and schooling. The *B and B Commission* had devoted one of its four volumes to *The Cultural Contribution of the Other Ethnic Groups* (Canada, Book IV, 1970) and the *Gendron Commission* followed suit with one entitled *The Ethnic Groups* (Quebec, Book III, 1972). Neither, however, pursued their analyses of pluralism in the terms discussed earlier in Chapter Two. Neither went beyond the limited and demographically linked concept of cultural pluralism. Both, on the other hand, saw the presence of groups of other than English or French backgrounds as *contributing* to an already established society, its culture and institutions.

Yet the questions above continued to be asked, and Allophones continued to resist concepts and models of society, culture and schooling based on assumptions with which they disagreed, and which failed to reflect contemporary realities. Thus J. B. Rudnyckyj, a Commissioner on the *B and B Commission*, filed without prejudice to the generality and validity of its *Report and Recommendations*, a separate statement dealing with supplementary considerations and additional recommendations that were necessary if the Report were to stand the test of time. He disagreed with the assumption that the words 'bilingualism and biculturalism' in the Commission's terms of reference meant French and English bilingualism and biculturalism. In his opinion, bilingualism implied an objective consideraton of all other forms of bilingualism in Canada including the position of regional languages; and in this respect, the Commission's suggested constitutional amendments were inadequate. What was needed, in addition to the designation of English and French as official languages, was the recognition of regional languages. These regional languages, moreover, were to be given preference in education as subjects or media of instruction at the elementary, high school and university levels (Canada, Book I, 1967: 155–169).

Allophone resistance to the English-French model of bilingualism and biculturalism played an influential part in shaping the federal government's bifurcated response to the recommendations of the *B and B Commission*. Official French–English bilingualism was translated into law in *The Official Languages Act* (1969) but biculturalism was not. Instead, with the support of all three political parties, a policy of *Multiculturalism Within a Bilingual*

Framework (1971) was announced. In presenting the policy in Parliament, Prime Minister Trudeau firmly rejected assimilation, deeming it an undesirable and unacceptable goal for Canadian society. The concept of the 'melting pot' was also considered inappropriate. It was the view of his government that

> there cannot be one cultural policy for Canadians of British and French origin, another for the original peoples and yet a third for all others. For although there are two official languages, there is no official culture, nor does any ethnic group take precedence over any other. No citizen or group of citizens is other than Canadian, and all should be treated fairly. (Trudeau, 1971: 1)

The policy expressed support for a number of goals: the presentation of basic human rights, the elimination of discrimination, the encouragement of cultural diversity, the strengthening of citizen participation, and the reinforcement of Canadian identity. It aimed at helping create a sense of identity, belonging and individual freedom of choice. These in turn were to form the basis of national unity. Ethnic loyalties, it was stressed, need not and usually did not, detract from wider loyalties to community and country.

Initial reception of the policy *Multiculturalism Within a Bilingual Framework* was at best mixed. Anglophones and a variety of other ethno-cultural groups seemed to favour it (Burnet, 1981). Francophones, on the other hand, expressed views ranging from lack of enthusiasm (Painchaud, 1976) to outright rejection (Rocher, 1972). The most vocal opposition was voiced by Francophones in Quebec who claimed that the new policy distorted both the historical and sociological realities of Canadian life. Canada, they argued vehemently, possessed two main cultures and two official languages. Moreover, as culture and language were indivisible, to juxtapose multiculturalism and bilingualism was contradictory. It was also politically dangerous, for the policy undermined the already slender faith of French-Canadians that the federal government was willing and able to protect their language and culture. Other critics consider the policy to be suspect on more narrow political grounds. As Reitz (1980) points out, ostensibly its political objective is the promotion of national unity through the strengthening of national allegiance, but more partisan political objectives have been charged. For example, the failure of the federal government's advisory committee, the Canadian Consultative Committee on Multiculturalism (CCMC), is said to have resulted from too close a relationship with the government party. It is alleged also that groups receiving financial support from the

Multiculturalism Directorate have been subject to manipulation and political management. In these and other ways, it is suggested, oppositional elements that might resist and challenge those things which hurt and oppress are marginalized (Thomas, 1984). The result is that minority ethno-cultural groups have been unable to establish organizations and institutions which could compete in any serious way with those of the two official language groups (Wardaugh, 1983).

> The ground for Canadian action can be traced to self-interest — a desire to palliate potentially disruptive minorities following radical accommodations to Francophone interest, and to the desire to incorporate minorities into a healthy capitalist economy. (Bagley, 1984: 8)

Analysts of the educational extension of the policy, or multicultural education as it is usually called, have varied in their support. Stock (1983: 25) views it as part of an attempt to alter the vertical mosaic 'through a process of attitude change directed at members of the two "charter groups" and at members of the non-French and non-British groups'. Stephan (1981–1983) observes that given their low priority and the limited funds accorded them, multicultural education policies have been seen as being designed to legitimize the *status quo*. Dehli (1984) is critical of the isolation of treatments of culture and education from economic realities, and gross imbalances of power among the different ethnic groups. Moodley (1984) is sceptical that the underlying assumption of cultural harmony which pervades most multicultural education programs will lead to any reduction of inequalities, or to a more equitable sharing of power.

Most analysts of multiculturalism are rightly critical of the lack of conceptual clarity surrounding the term. There is, too, a strong sense that its intellectual foundations are shaky and that there is a considerable need for more full-blown, rigorous analyses. These concerns apply with equal if not more weight to the field of multicultural education. Is multicultural education a socio-political instrument for ensuring cooperation by granting limited concessions? (Stephan, 1981–1983). Is it designed to realize democratic ideals or is it another form of social control? (Barton & Walker, 1983). Is the cultural capital minority children bring to school to be viewed as different but valid, or inappropriate and deficient? Are multicultural educational materials included for therapeutic purposes? Do they celebrate individual social mobility but ignore ethnic stratification? Do they stress consensus and avoid dealing with conflict? (Manicom, 1984). Do they assume knowledge will reduce prejudice and discrimination? Do present priorities recognize and legitimize cultural differences while failing to deal with racism at the institutional and structural as well as individual level? (Patel, 1980). Or as some argue, do current approaches help maintain the myth about minority groups as 'problems to be studied' while leaving institutional and structural inequalities intact? (Augustine, 1984).

Conclusion

During the 1970s the three versions of Canadian culture we have examined each had their impact on schools. Assimilation continued to exert an influence on practice despite being rejected at the level of policy (Young, 1983). Multiculturalism, as we have just seen, attracted some attention and support. But it was the second of the three models, bilingualism and biculturalism, that dominated. Efforts to translate it into programmatic, institutional and structural forms met with considerable opposition which on occasion erupted into bitter conflict and struggle (Sylvestre, 1980).

In a number of the provinces, educational applications of the bilingual–bicultural model were strongly opposed by Anglophone majorities. Some liberalization of 'what were in 1966 very restrictive policies with respect to minority language education' in Ontario, Manitoba and New Brunswick (Rideout, 1977: 132) took place, but progress elsewhere was slow. Only in New Brunswick, Canada's only officially bilingual province, can it be said that considerable progress was made. Here a new Schools Act (1978) included the following provisions:

(a) School districts, schools and classes shall be organized on one or other of the official languages.
(b) The Minister of Education may establish, on her/his own initiative, with the approval of the Lieutenant-Governor in Council, in any school district in addition to the existing school board, a school board for the official language group in that school district whose language is not the official language on the basis of which the school district is organized.
(c) Alternatively, the Minister shall establish in a school district, where parents
    (i)   who reside in that school district,
    (ii) whose language is the official language which is not the official language on the basis of which the school is organized, and

(iii) who are the parents of not less than thirty children of elementary school age, submit a request in accordance with the regulations, a school board for the official language group in that school district whose language is not the language on the basis of which the school district is organized within six months of receipt by the Minister of such a request.

(d) In any school district where a minority language school board is not in existence, but where there is a minority of persons whose language is one of the official languages, the Minister, with the approval of the Lieutenant-Governor in Council, may establish an advisory committee representative of that minority to advise the school board of that district with respect to the education of the pupils forming a part of that minority of persons. (New Brunswick Schools Act, 1978).

By 1981, the above provisions had radically altered the previous school system. Two systems in fact had come into existence: one was English-language and the other French-language. The English-language system consisted of 25 school boards while those in the French-language system numbered 12. All told, 150,000 students were enrolled in grades 1 through 12, two-thirds of whom attended English-language schools, and one-third French-language schools (Malmberg, 1981).

The absence of substantial progress in institutional and structural terms elsewhere, coupled with the restrictive nature of Clause 73 in Bill 101, undoubtedly fueled efforts to enshrine official language educational rights in a new Canadian Constitution. In 1981, these efforts were rewarded with the inclusion of minority language educational rights in the *Canadian Charter of Rights and Freedoms*, which formed part of the *Constitution Act* (1982). Section 23 of the Charter, 'Minority Language Educational Rights', contains the following provisions:

Minority Language Educational Rights
23(1) Citizens of Canada
     (a) whose first language learned and still understood is that of the English or French linguistic minority population of the province in which they reside, or
     (b) who have received their primary school instruction in Canada in English or French and reside in a province where the language in which they received that instruction is the language of the English or French linguistic minority population of the province,

have the right to have their children receive primary and secondary school instruction in that language in that province.

23(2) Citizens of Canada of whom any child has received or is receiving primary or secondary school instruction in English or French in Canada, have the right to have all their children receive primary and secondary school instruction in the same language.

23(3) The right of citizens of Canada under subsection (1) and (2) to have their children receive primary and secondary school instruction in the language of the English or French linguistic minority population of a province

(a) applies wherever in the province the number of children of citizens who have such a right is sufficient to warrant the provision to them out of public funds of minority language intruction; and

(b) includes, where the number of those children so warrants, the right to have them receive that instruction in minority language educational facilities provided out of public funds.

Interpretations of these provisions (see Chapter Five) are still being developed. Notwithstanding the fact that access to minority language education is now a constitutional right rather than a provision subject to the possibility of legislative change, the translation of this right into practice is somewhat halting. Why is this the case? Why have the bilingual–bicultural model, and the legislative and constitutional efforts to implement it, experienced such difficulty in gaining acceptance? Conclusive answers, especially with regard to the eventual impact of the new *Constitution Act* (1982), are not available, but a number of problems with the model can be identified.

To begin with, the model's assumptions do not adequately reflect the demographic, economic and political changes that have occurred since Confederation, and especially since World War II. As a result, the concepts and terminology employed in the model are of limited applicability. Concepts such as 'charter groups' and 'founding peoples' are considered suspect and are frequently rejected out of hand. Native peoples consider the concept of 'founding peoples' to be inaccurate, inappropriate and even insulting. Members of minority racial and ethnocultural groups, particularly in Western Canada, dislike both this term and the concept of 'charter groups'. They also resent the appellation 'other ethnic groups', which to many smacks of marginalization, subordinate status, and second-class citizenship.

No more has the compromise or hybrid model of multiculturalism within a bilingual framework satisfied the heterogeneous aspirations and expectations of Canada's multiracial, multiethnic population. In the absence of acceptable and appropriate integrating institutions and structures, therefore, it is hardly surprising that conflicts over culture and schooling continue to form some of the major issues of our time. It is to a treatment of three of these that the next chapter is devoted. By describing and analysing these issues, it is hoped that our understanding of the plural nature of contemporary Canada can be enhanced, and the possibilities of alternative forms of schooling explored.

5 Contemporary issues

Introduction

The three major issues that are examined in this chapter illustrate the contested nature of Canadian pluralism and its reflection in disputes over culture and schooling. They emphasize the limited, general applicability in the contemporary context of the three models of Canadian society and culture discussed in the previous chapter, and reinforce the importance of current efforts aimed at identifying and developing appropriate understandings and forms. Canadian cultural institutions and structures — especially in the area of education — are seen for what they are: the outcomes of contests between dominant and subordinate cultural groups. These contests, and the struggles to which they give rise, it is emphasized, are not isolated events. On the contrary, they are centrally located in the legal, economic, political and social framework of Canadian society.

Aboriginal rights: Self-governance

Perhaps no single issue illuminates the contested nature of culture in Canada more than the governance of state-supported schools. In this respect the current and controversial constitutional debates over the nature of aboriginal self-government are of particular interest, for they provide valuable insights into the relationship between culture and schooling in a plural society. The fundamental issues raised, the questions involved, the processes, structural models and institutional forms under consideration all possess implications beyond the immediate issues involved. They go to the heart of concerns which many subordinate groups experience regarding their participation in policy-setting and decision-making. They lie at the centre of minority group struggles to exercise control over the future development of their cultures. They seek, in a very direct way, to interpret what is understood by group and parental rights to educate.

The history of schooling for the aboriginal peoples in Canada, while containing individual instances of success, is for the most part a record of continuing, systematic failure (Burnaby, 1979). Since 1867, the federal government and its agents have abrogated the right of aboriginal governments to make all decisions affecting their people (Boisvert, 1985). First the church and later the state established residential or boarding schools for native students which detached them from their communities, families, culture, language, belief systems and life-styles. Native children were to be isolated, proselytized and introduced to the benefits of Euro-Canadian civilization in a concerted effort to eradicate and replace their indigenous culture and language. Only over the last 25 years or so has the structural pattern of native schools operated by the churches, but funded primarily by the state, been set aside. Yet even today, 54% of Indian children commute to provincial and private schools from their homes on the reserves (Canadian Education Association, 1984). As well, assimilationist practices, especially in the area of language, while not overtly sanctioned at the policy level, continue to be vigorously pursued (Tschanz, 1980). Indian participation on school boards is still rare and is generally limited to membership on native advisory committees (the power of appointment resting with the school board) or to native education councils on the reserves. The majority of school boards enrolling native children still do not have a policy regarding native representation. While in some school boards the need for native content and instruction in the native languages is receiving much-needed attention, it is all too clear that in many others nothing is being done (Canadian Education Authority, 1984: 84).

That the assimilationist efforts of schools to replace native language and culture have failed to achieve their goal is frequently explained by means of deficit theory. That is, it is argued that native children fail to achieve conventional academic success because they are culturally and linguistically deficient. Explanations are rarely couched in terms of the inability of the school system to provide an education that builds on and reinforces the cultural capital the children already possess. Nor are the longstanding efforts of native communities to resist cultural impoverishment and replacement often taken into account. Yet this resistance can help explain the school system's failure to maintain adequate retention rates and levels of achievement among native children. It can help explain the persistence of native cultures in the face of assimilationist pressures, and it can contribute to our understanding of the revival of native efforts to reassert their treaty and aboriginal rights.

The rejection of assimilationist policies, the need for change, and the provision of an alternative philosophy of native education were dramatically asserted in the seminal document *Indian Control of Indian Education* published by the National Indian Brotherhood in 1972. The National Indian Brotherhood categorically rejected the *B and B Commission*'s position that British and French cultures should dominate in the public schools. In its view, the school's primary responsibility towards native children was to reinforce their cultural identity. They needed to learn their own history, values, customs and language, if they were to take pride in that identity. To achieve these goals, given the past and present performance of state-aided schools, the hegemonic control of the white majority must be set aside and authority for native education placed firmly in the hands of the native peoples themselves. Over the last decade some slight progress has been made in this direction, but it is hampered by the very fact that the authorities who presently control native education and are charged with transferring this control, are essentially participating in the dissolution of the organizational units to which they belong.

All existing forms of self-government in aboriginal education are subordinate in that the authority these forms possess consists of powers delegated to them by a superordinate level of government: federal, provincial or territorial. Thus the delegating power controls what it decides to delegate and can alter or reverse the same. Currently the *Indian Act* recognizes two forms of Indian government on reserves: traditional leadership and a form of Indian administration called a Band Council. Indian bands can choose either form, but not both, and the majority of bands have opted for band councils. The Minister, however, and through him his department, reserves the authority to approve anything the Band Council does and to overrule it if need be.

Indian education authorities operate 187 on-reserve schools providing educational services for 13,000 students or just over 16% of the Indian student population. As part of the James Bay and Northern Quebec Agreement, the Inuit, Cree and Nashapi peoples assumed administrative control of their respective school systems and, by virtue of the granting of special powers, have been able to adapt them to their cultural and linguistic needs and aspirations. In British Columbia, as part of their comprehensive claims negotiations, the Nishga Indians are seeking control over education and the Nishga School Board has been created under provincial law. Saskatchewan has experimented with regional local councils in the northern half of the province which are, to all intents and purposes, controlled by the Metis and Non-Status Indians (Boisvert, 1985). And in Manitoba, seven Indian Tribal Councils have been established representing 57 bands and 44,000 Indians. Each Tribal Council is made up of several Bands that have formally united to facilitate the transfer to local control of federal government powers and responsibilities for education.

In urban centres, native schools are rare but at least three are currently operating. Wandering Spirit Survival School was established in 1976 under the jurisdiction of the City of Toronto Board of Education. The school stresses the spiritual and cultural heritage of its students, along with basic academic skills. Operating policies and procedures are determined by an all-Native Council on which parents, students and school supporters sit. In the Plains Indian Cultural Survival School, founded in 1979 under the auspices of the Calgary Board of Education, native languages are taught, and students spend 40% of their time pursuing cultural activities taught by Band elders. A similar institution, the Saskatoon Native Survival School, was started in 1980 as a cooperative project between the Native School Society, the Saskatoon Catholic School Board and the Saskatchewan Department of Education.

To date, calls for self-government in education for aboriginal peoples have reached their most sophisticated expression (if not widespread implementation) in the Northwest Territories, the population of which is composed of four major cultural groups: Inuit, Dene, Metis and Euro-Canadians. However, even here developments fall within the category of administrative bodies possessing delegated executive powers, and these powers too are limited. In the Northwest Territories, 'bilingualism' usually means Inuktitut-English, Slavey-English, Dogrib-English, Loucheux-English, Chipewyan-English or Inuvialuktun-English. Here too, aboriginal communities have criticized the government for operating a school system that seems unable to keep children in school or to assist them to progress to higher levels of education. Thus, for example, the

> leadership of the Dene Nation has been concerned for some years about ways in which the Dene of the Mackenzie Valley can control the education of their children so that Dene cultural and constitutional aspirations are realized and so that the young people of the Dene Nation are prepared to control and administer the institutions which will flow from federal recognition of Dene aboriginal rights. (Dene Nation, 1984: 1)

While the Dene recognize that much more work and research needs to be done before substantive proposals on Dene control of Dene education can be presented to the territorial and federal governments, they are clearly concerned that they do not control the funds set out for education. In addition, three possible options have been identified. The first consists of the development and implementation of the Dene educational process, including Dene-trained teachers and Dene-developed curriculum materials, within the existing territorial educational system. The second involves organizing communities in such a way that the whole community functions as a centre for learning, rather than just having learning centred within a school building, in order that the learning needs of all Dene (not just the young people) might be met. The third would lead to the establishment of a separate educational system run by the Dene themselves (Dene Nation, 1984: 3).

The government of the Northwest Territories currently governs the school system through its Department of Education and has recently adopted an explicit pluralist philosophy of education. Multiculturalism is stressed and bilingualism is interpreted to mean both official and aboriginal languages. In an attempt to satisfy the many language development needs, the government has recognized two principles as the basis for the development of future language programs: support for bilingual education (English/Aboriginal languages) and the rights of communities to decide on native language programs and how they should be developed. Normative outcomes include the expectation that a high school graduate would be able to demonstrate 'a knowledge of his/her own cultural background and an understanding of the multi-cultural, multiethnic nature of the Northwest Territories in particular, and of Canada in general' (Northwest Territories Department of Education, 1978: 1).

In order to reinforce these normative goals, a number of innovative structures have been constructed. Depending upon local and regional conditions, the local education authority may be either a community education committee, a community education society, or a regional educational society or authority. Effective 1st April, 1985, in the Baffin region only, Community Education Councils will replace committees and societies, and a Divisional Board of Education will replace the Baffin Region Educational Society. These structures are all community-based and are designed to ensure that minority cultures shape the policies, curricula, staffing and operating procedures of publicly-funded schools. As such, they are being watched carefully by aboriginal groups and their organizations both within the Northwest Territories and beyond. Attention, in particular, is being paid to the question of fiscal control.

According to one knowledgeable observer, working models of aboriginal education require guarantees in both primary and subordinate legislation to prevent distortion of appropriate policies and procedures. In his view, the

> absolute democratization of Indian Education can only be possible under terms of *absolute* control of funding; the bottom line to all current transfer-to-local control projects is that the feds still hold the purse strings.

Without control of these purse strings, it will be difficult if not impossible to establish 'functional democracy' as opposed to the 'guided democracy' of the past (Couture, 1979).

In addition to the critical scrutiny of existing and alternative policies and structures in native education, legal research is being carried out on the interpretation of education clauses in various treaties. Research on the *James Bay Treaty* (1905), for example, undertaken by the Nishnawbe-Aski Nation, has focused on the wording of the education clause which reads as follows:

> Further, His Majesty agrees to pay such salaries to teachers to instruct the children of said Indians, and also to provide such school buildings and educational equipment as may seem advisable to His Majesty's Government in Canada. (Cheechoo, 1985: 1)

This wording, which is similar to that of education clauses in many other Indian treaties, is being interpreted to mean, first, that the clause provides an absolute guarantee of teacher salaries; second, that the federal government is obligated to provide school buildings and equipment; and third, that Indians under the treaty enjoy a bilateral relationship with Canada and the federal government, which is identified as the provider of educational services to the exclusion of the province of Ontario.

Based on the fact that Canadian courts have previously treated Indian treaties as perpetual but flexible agreements and have interpreted them liberally, three further interpretations have been

1. The word 'children' employed in 1905 would today include university students, might include adult training, and might guarantee education outside the geographical boundaries covered by the treaty.
2. Nothing in the clause gives either the federal or the provincial government the right to destroy Indian culture through control of educational programs. On the contrary, the clause enshrines Canada's constitutional duty to preserve and enhance all aspects of Indian culture, including language.

3. Nothing in the clause undermines self-government in education. The federal government is obliged to fund staff, facilities and equipment but each band retains sovereignty over curriculum structure, etc. Further, the bilateral nature of the treaty requires that the consent of the Nishnawbe-Aski must be obtained before the federal government may delegate any educational matter to Ontario (Cheecho, 1985: 3–4).

The Nishnawbe-Aski nation also argues that the federal government has delegated many matters in education to the provincial government of Ontario without seeking its permission; that the guarantee of educational benefits is an 'existing' right; and that the federal government has lost the capacity (under the new constitution) to abrogate 'existing' treaty rights unilaterally.

Challenges to the *status quo* (such as the above), together with existing expressions of aboriginal participation in various forms of self-government in education, provide partial answers to the question 'What do aboriginal peoples want?' Similarly, although there is no agreement on specifics, the aboriginal peoples generally believe that in order to survive as distinct cultures or peoples they need a land base and self-government. This means reaffirming and reinforcing their power to exist as distinct collectivities and requires the power to exercise their collective rights. Aboriginal peoples want these powers not only to protect native identities but also to enable them to improve social and public services by exercising control over matters such as education, language and other cultural areas (Boisvert, 1985). All four aboriginal peoples' organizations — the Assembly of First Nations, the Inuit Committee on National Issues, the Native Council of Canada, and the Metis National Council — view self-government as an inherent right. Moreover, and this needs to be stressed, all four advocate self-government within the Canadian political system (Hawkes, 1985).

It is within this context that controversies over the substance and process of the current constitutional negotiations on aboriginal rights can best be understood. Section 35 of the *Constitution Act* (1982), as we have seen, recognized and reaffirmed the existing aboriginal and treaty rights of the native peoples of Canada, and Section 37 provided for the convening of a constitutional conference to deal with 'constitutional matters that directly affect the aboriginal peoples of Canada, including the identification and definition of the rights of those peoples to be included in the Constitution of Canada . . .' Representatives of the aboriginal peoples, the federal and provincial governments, and where deemed appropriate by the

Prime Minister, elected representatives of the Yukon Territory and the Northwest Territories, were invited to participate in the conference. First convened in 1983, the conference has also met in 1984 and 1985. One issue has come to dominate all of its discussions: aboriginal self-government.

It is important to remember that there are two thrusts to any policy on aboriginal self-government: the enhancement of aboriginal representation in the policy-making processes of the state, and enhanced autonomy for aboriginal peoples to manage their own affairs. The 'first important variable involved with forms of self-government for the aboriginal peoples is the authority function — the kind and degree of authority that are recognized within the political system' (Boisvert, 1985: 17). While the four national aboriginal peoples' organizations favour the entrenchment of aboriginal self-government in the Constitution, the same degree of unanimity does not apply to the thirteen governments participating in the constitutional conference. The federal government has gone on record in 1984 in recognizing the aboriginal right to self-government; six of the other governments favour entrenching in the Constitution some form of principle on aboriginal self-government, autonomy of self-determination; seven are split between having no position and questioning the need to entrench the principle in the Constitution (Hawkes, 1985). To date, no agreement has been reached on what is meant by aboriginal self-government. Its definition will likely emerge as the constitutional talks continue. However, it is generally agreed that the concept includes issues of education, language and culture as well as those of land title, resources and economic development. It is generally agreed, too, that whatever forms of aboriginal self-government are finally adopted, they will stop short of complete sovereignty and reflect a qualified form of autonomy.

The major constitutional controversy over aboriginal self-government centers on the forms it would take *vis-à-vis* existing governments. Three approaches are currently being discussed: delegation, devolution and constitutional entrenchment. The first, delegation, is unpopular with many of the native peoples; there are as well limits to delegation in Canadian federalism. The second, devolution, lies somewhere mid-way between delegation and constitutional entrenchment; it suggests turning responsibility for managing their own affairs over to the native peples, and 'implies an irrevocability to transfers of jurisdiction which is absent from the delegation model' (Boisvert, 1985: 72). The third, constitutional entrenchment, which is unacceptable to many of the governments, involves amending the Constitution to recognize collective rights such as the right of aboriginal peoples to educate their own children, speak their own language, control their own membership and manage their own collective property.

What powers, authority and models of aboriginal self-government might eventually be agreed upon are questions to which the answers vary considerably. Exclusive aboriginal participation is most easily secured in interest-group-like institutional arrangements at the local government level. However, the aboriginal peoples, being no more homogeneous than other Canadians, have no single model in mind. There are many possible forms of models, and their jurisdictional scope may vary widely depending upon the history and traditions of the groups involved (Boisvert, 1985). They have developed their notions of self-government with varying degrees of detail and clarity and these range from broad concepts of 'nationhood' to specific suggestions regarding local school boards. Nor do the various governments involved have a clear idea of what models they might be willing to accept. Certain provincial governments, for example, are much more amenable than others toward granting self-government as expressed in terms of either: (a) regional ethnic government with autonomous or semi-autonomous power at least some of which would be legislative rather than merely administrative; or (b) local ethnic government with autonomous powers, which are legislative (Hawkes, 1985).

Local ethnic government with dependent powers primarily of an administrative nature, of which existing Indian band governments are an example, is clearly a non-starter. In this model, local government powers would be essentially administrative and confined to such areas as culture, education and language funded for the most part through conditional grants. Local ethnic government with semi-autonomous powers, some of which are legislative, is currently being explored in Quebec. An inter-governmental agreement in 1984 between the provincial government and the Kahnawake Mohawks, for example, included a clause recognizing the right of aboriginal nations to have and control institutions in such areas as culture, education and health.

Local ethnic government with substantial autonomy is similar to the model of self-government proposed by The Assembly of First Nations and is the preferred option of three of the four national peoples' organizations. It also most closely approximates the model recommended in the report of the House of Commons Special Committee on Indian Self-Government, popularly known as the *Penner Report*. This report recommended, in addition to entrenching the right of Indian people to self-government in the Constitution, that Indian First Nations governments with substantial legislative powers be recognized through an Act of Parliament (Hawkes,

1985). More generally, it is worth noting that, in discussions of proposals for aboriginal self-government, it is common to differentiate between those that apply to regions above and below the sixtieth parallel. Proposals in the Northwest Territories, for instance, do not have to consider the provinces since no provinces exist in that area, whereas proposals for aboriginal government made south of sixty must consider that any jurisdiction they exercise will have a direct impact not only on the federal government but on provincial governments as well (Boisvert, 1985).

Discussions of the various models proposed in the talks are continuing. Agreement on self-government, even in principle, however, has not been reached. Negotiations are also continuing between the federal government and the Assembly of First Nations regarding a successor to Bill C-52, legislation designed to establish Indian self-government. In the Yukon and Northwest Territories trilateral negotiations on land claims settlements, which include provisions for Inuit, Metis and Indian self-government, are taking place. In the meantime, the gap between the perceptions and expectations of aboriginal peoples and Canadian governments may be unprecedented.

> The profound differences in values and perspectives between aboriginal tribal and traditional views and European-Canadian views cannot be understated. Not only are the 'mind sets' foreign to one another, but so too are the languages and concepts. (Hawkes, 1985: 85)

Nor is there agreement on process. Section 37's process is fraught with problems. All seventeen parties appear to be rethinking the political process, and many are considering a set of parallel negotiations at the regional or provincial level to supplement and feed into the national process.

Despite the difficulties, a number of significant points have already emerged from the constitutional talks. The most important of these is the general political recognition at the governmental level of the necessity of aboriginal peoples to possess some form of self-government if they are to participate in Canadian economic, political and social life, while at the same time possessing the necessary autonomy and self-determination to develop their cultures. Recognition alone, of course, as the example of the United States reveals, is by itself no cure for the problems of aboriginal dependency. Establishment of land and revenue bases are major concerns that have been identified. A land base is necessary to develop a viable economy, and several measures regarding the development of a revenue base can be considered: the management of treaty entitlements, trust funds and other capital funds; tax exemption; revenue sharing and taxing power (Boisvert, 1985). In addition, as Hawkes (1985) has pointed out there is considerable evidence that

> the drive of aboriginal peoples for self-government will not be snuffed out. Failure would merely strengthen their resolve. Demands on governments to recognize aboriginal rights to self-government will not decrease, but increase. Public opinion and support for aboriginal peoples will not fall away, but will grow. (Hawkes, 1985: 97)

There is no going back. In recognizing a right to self-government we are concerned not with what exists, but with establishing new institutions so that aboriginal peoples can make their own collective decisions. Possible avenues include local aboriginal governments, regional government, municipal government, national aboriginal special purpose bodies, regional aboriginal special purpose bodies, band council government, aboriginal representation in national and regional governments, and even regional aboriginal governments. Aboriginal laws could be made paramount and concurrent in at least specific fields such as cultural, social and educational policy. There is no reason, as Boisvert (1985) points out, why we could not experiment with all these forms at once to meet different situations across the country. No single approach or model will meet the aspiration of all aboriginal peoples. Any attempt to apply 'universal' models, processes or legal instruments would be ill-advised. A flexible approach will have to be developed to accommodate diverse structures and allocations of policy responsiblilty (Hawkes, 1985). This last point applies with particular force to cultural, linguistic and educational policy if the current absence of native participation in the education of their children is to be reversed and their cultural identity maintained and enhanced.

Official language minority educational rights

The second major current issue highlighting the contested and conflicting nature of culture and schooling in Canada is that of official language minority educational rights. This particular issue has attracted more political, constitutional and legal controversy than any other single issue in recent years. And while our discussion of aboriginal self-government confirms the limited applicability of the English–French, bilingual–bicultural model, the furor over minority language educational rights underlines the model's continuing importance in Canada's efforts to articulate and implement an appropriate set of cultural assumptions and structures.

The issue of minority language educational rights is particularly significant for it powerfully illuminates the complex nature of dominant–subordinate relations (English–French, French–English), emphasizes their essential dynamism and demonstrates conclusively that conflicts over schooling are inextricably linked to the larger political, economic and social context of the Canadian state. In addition, as did the issue of governance, it reinforces the fact that subordinate groups are seeking structural as well as institutional reflections of their cultures and languages in publicly-funded systems of education.

Cultural, political and constitutional struggles in the area of official language minority rights have attracted much attention of late among social scientists (Bourhis, 1984). Legal scholars, too, are participating in growing numbers as efforts to resolve the conflicts over educational rights find their way into the highest courts of the land. Indeed the courts are now engaged in the formulation and definition of educational policy to an unprecedented degree. This explains why the approach adopted in the following pages focuses almost exclusively on recent developments in the legal and constitutional spheres, for it is there that the tense drama of official language minority educational rights is being played out.

We begin our consideration of the legal ramifications of the issue with a reminder that the courts have historically played a role in determining minority language educational rights. In 1912, for example, the courts not only upheld the validity of Regulation 17 in Ontario, which placed stringent restrictions on the use of French as a language of instruction, but also reserved to the legislature of that province the 'power to mold the educational system in the interest of the public at large' (Magnet, 1982: 198). Francophone minorities outside Quebec lacked the power to protect their language and 'accordingly were unable to put into place a network of institutions consonant with their culture' (Leslie, 1984: 9). Their only protection was the good will of the Anglophone majority, and in a number of instances this was singularly lacking (Brown, 1969; Monnin, 1983). Large-scale linguistic assimilation was the result, and contemporary policies designed to revive the French language in Anglo-Canada have been insufficient to stem the tide of anglicization amongst Francophone minorities outside Quebec (Bourhis, 1984).

It was against this background and with prior judgements from other provinces in mind that Chief Justice Deschenes dismissed a challenge to

Quebec's *Official Language Act* (Bill 22) by the Protestant Board of Montreal:

> When the constitutional test was similar, did anyone think of serving the French culture of the Catholic minority of Manitoba, when the language question was underlying the religious conflict which was jeopardizing its right to denominational schools? And when the constitutional test was identical did anyone think of serving the French culture of the Catholic minority of Ontario when the language question also jeopardized its system of denominational schools?

> At each of these solemn moments in our history the Courts have distinguished between language and faith, between culture and religion, they have recognized constitutional guarantees to the denomination of schools only and never did they interpret the British North America Act, 1867, as an instrument of the protection of the language or the culture of a particular group ((1978), 83 D.L.R. (3d) 645 at 672, 673).

The failure of the *British North America Act* (1867) to provide and protect schooling in the official languages, taken together with the passage of Bill 101 in Quebec, gave added impetus to ultimately successful efforts to have minority language education rights constitutionally enshrined in Clause 23 of the *Canadian Charter of Rights and Freedoms* (1982).

Within Quebec the conflict over which of the two took precedence — the *Charter of the French Language* (Bill 101) or the Canadian Charter of Rights and Freedoms — quickly focused on the conflict between Clause 23(1)(b) in the latter and Section 73 in the former. Thus Clause 23(1) (b) became known as the 'Canadian clause' and Section 73 the 'Quebec clause'. The latter, it will be recalled, refused admission to schools in which the language of instruction was English, to children of English-speaking parents who had received their education in another Canadian province. The matter was not long in coming to a head. The Quebec Association of Protestant School Boards brought suit against the Attorney-General of Quebec claiming that Section 73 of Bill 101 was unconstitutional. This case was also heard by Chief Justice Deschenes, who ruled that the 'Quebec clause' was of no force and effect insofar as it was inconsistent with Section 23 of the Canadian Charter of Rights and Freedoms (1983), 140 D.L.R. (3d) 33.

In making his judgement Chief Justice Deschenes reached a number of important conclusions. First, he concluded that one of the most important effects of an entrenched *Charter of Rights and Freedoms* was that it changed the 'rules of the game', giving the courts a significant degree of legislative power. Second, being conscious of what was at stake and aware that the court was exercising authority in a new and difficult field, he concluded that the *Charter* ought not to be interpreted too narrowly. The whole thrust of constitutional law was aimed at ensuring liberal interpretations and generous and uniform applications. Third, he emphasized that with respect to the language of instruction, the *Charter* recognized individual rights and not collective rights. And fourth, he stressed the fact that he had reached his judgement quite independently of the results that might ensue. These were not a matter for the courts, but properly belonged to the realm of politics.

The Quebec government appealed Deschene's decision. The Quebec Court of Appeal unanimously rejected the government's argument that the Quebec clause did nothing more than to impose limitations upon s. 23 *Charter* rights, and that these limitations were reasonable and thus permitted by s. 1 of the *Charter*. The Court dismissed the appeal in short order and with brief reasons, and a further appeal was filed in the Supreme Court of Canada (*Quebec Association of Protestant School Boards et al. v. Attorney-General of Quebec et al. (No. 2) (1984)*, 7 C.R.R. 139). Here again the Quebec government argued that Bill 101 was constitutional in that it imposed reasonable limits on the rights of Anglophones; even within Quebec itself the French language was threatened and thus the legislature had a responsibility to promote and protect it. Lawyers for the federal government and the Protestant school boards countered by arguing that the 'Quebec clause' prohibited Anglophone parents from sending a child to an English-language school unless one of them had received his or her primary instruction in English in the province, and that this violated the *Charter*. The government of New Brunswick also appeared before the Court as an intervenor with a brief submitting that, under Section 23 of the *Charter*, citizens educated in English or French in Canada had the right to educate their children in the same language anywhere in the country (*Attorney-General of Quebec v. Quebec Association of Protestant School Boards*, (1984), 9 C.R.R. 133).

The case is of great significance because it marked one of the first times under the *Charter* that the Supreme Court had been required to determine the extent to which a government could limit an individual's constitutional rights, on the one hand, and the power of the courts to overrule legislation, on the other. The lawyer for the Quebec government argued that the court should not overrule the decision of elected representatives. The lawyer for the federal government argued that the

Charter must be given a broad and liberal interpretation that will benefit those on whom it confers rights. Thus the Court should uphold the ruling of the lower courts in Quebec and strike down those provisions of Bill 101 on English language education that violated the *Charter*. On 26th July, 1984, the Supreme Court ruled unanimously that Bill 101's restrictions on schooling for the children of citizens of Canada educated in English elsewhere in Canada were 'inoperable' and 'inconsistent' with the *Charter*.

A second significant court case dealing with official language minority educational rights had been heard by the Court of Appeal in Ontario a year earlier. In this case, the central point at issue was the right of the French-language minority to representation on local school boards. Such representation had been proposed earlier in an Ontario government White Paper (1983) which recommended amendments to *The Education Act* (1980) giving responsibility for direction of minority language instruction to a minority section of the board of school trustees. The proposal proved highly controversial and, in an effort to defuse and resolve the issue, the Lieutenant-Governor-in-Council referred the matter to the Court of Appeal for its constitutional opinion.

More specifically, the Court was asked to give its opinion on four questions regarding the constitutional validity of certain provisions of the Ontario *Education Act* (1980) and of proposals to amend it contained in the White Paper dated March 23, 1983. The questions read as follows:

1. Are sections 258 and 261 of the *Education Act* inconsistent with the *Canadian Charter of Rights and Freedoms* and, if so, in what particular or particulars and to what extent?
2. Is the *Education Act* inconsistent with the *Canadian Charter of Rights and Freedoms* in that members of the French linguistic minority in Ontario entitled to have their children receive instruction in the French language are not accorded the right to manage and control their own French language classes of instruction and French language educational facilities?
3. Do minority-language educational rights in the *Canadian Charter of Rights and Freedoms* apply with equal force and effect to minority language instruction and educational facilities provided for denominational education under Parts IV and V of the *Education Act* and to minority language instruction and educational facilities provided for public education under the *Education Act*?

4. Is it within the legislative authority of the Legislative Assembly of Ontario to amend the *Education Act* as contemplated in the White Paper of March 23, 1983, in relation to boards of education, to provide for the election of minority-language trustees to Roman Catholic separate school boards to exercise certain exclusive responsibilities as minority-language sections of such school boards?

In reaching its decisions on these four questions, the Ontario Court of Appeal determined that the *Charter* was intended to be interpreted liberally and generously. In addition, it observed:

> The preservation and enforcement of the guaranteed rights including minority language educational rights, and of fundamental freedoms have changed the focus of constitutional law and the role of the courts. We believe that the Court's concern for these rights requires a move away from narrow and strict constructionalism toward a broader approach, which would include a consideration of the historical developments, particularly in the field of education ((1984), 47 O.R. (2d) 1).

With this in mind, and setting out the particulars in its detailed judgement, the Court found that Sections 258 and 261 were inconsistent with the *Charter* to the extent set out. Minority language education rights should not be left to the unfettered and undirected discretion of local school boards 'no matter how competent and well meaning they may be'. The proposals giving responsibility for direction of minority language instruction to a minority-speaking section of the board of trustees appeared 'to be no different in kind from other major structural changes made in such boards from time to time since 1867'. The *Charter*'s minority language educational rights applied with equal force and effect to both denominational and public educations.

According to the Court, the following degree of participation and control met the requirements of the *Charter*:

> ... representation of the linguistic minority on local boards or other public authorities which administer minority language instruction or facilities should be guaranteed;

> ... those representatives should be given exclusive authority to make decisions pertaining to the provision of minority language instruction and facilities within their jurisdiction, including the expenditure of the funds provided for such instruction and facilities, and the appointment and direction of those responsible for the administration of such

instruction and facilities.

Enforcement of the minority's right to French language education, moreover, should not be left to the courts on applications alleging infringement of *Charter* rights. Rather, in the Court's opinion, minority linguistic rights in the future should be established by general legislation. What the Court did not determine was the meaning of key words and phrases in Section 23 such as 'instruction', 'where numbers warrant', 'educational facilities' and 'out of public funds'.

The Court did, however, offer some hints as to its thinking on these matters. It found provisions in the existing *Education Act*, with regard to numbers (25 for primary schools and 20 for secondary schools), to be too rigid and inconsistent with the *Charter*. It also considered the *Charter* to contemplate something more than the presence of French-speaking teachers in classrooms in which French-speaking children were taught. Drawing attention to Section 27 (the Multiculturalism clause) of the *Charter*, it observed that Section 23(3)(b)

> should be interpreted to mean that minority language children must receive their instruction in facilities in which the educational environment will be that of the linguistic minority. Only then can the facilities reasonably be said to reflect the minority culture and appertain to the minority. ((1984), 47 O.R. (2d) 1)

Precise definitions of Section 23's key words and phrases probably await judgments on motions such as that filed at the Court of Queen's Bench in Alberta in October, 1983, seeking an interpretation of Section 23 as to issues of numbers, public funding and creation of Francophone school boards (Martel, 1984). Presently, different numbers trigger the provision of minority French-language instruction in different provinces, and it may well be that the definition of the number of students necessary to receive instruction in minority language educational facilities will continue to vary. Definitions, for example, could be based on numbers required to establish either a class or a program or school. The provinces could also broaden access beyond the requirements of Section 23.

If the exigencies of Section 23 are to be satisfied, a right to 'instruction' accrues. If a further numbers test is met, then that instruction must be received in 'minority language educational facilities'. This phrase, it has been suggested, implies something beyond the provision of instruction; it envisages control over the administration and operation of minority language schools. It is reasonable to assume that this administration and operation would be carried on in the minority language. Interpretations of Section 23 might also require the establishment of minority language school boards (or other vehicles of self-governance) in areas where minority numbers are especially concentrated — even if existing school districts have to be redrawn (Magnet, 1982). Court action, for example, is being considered by *L'Association des Enseignants Franco-Ontariens* in an attempt to give French-speaking residents control of all Francophone schools (OSTC, 21–25 January, 1985).

A major criticism of provincial efforts to comply with Section 23 of the *Charter* by amending education legislation is that for the most part the provincial legislation does not go far enough. Section 23, it is argued, imposes an obligation on the provinces to provide education as prescribed, and anything less than legislation which will guarantee such provision amounts to a contravention of the *Charter* (Foucher, 1985). Of all the provinces, only New Brunswick has legislation which imposes on the Minister a positive obligation to act. Elsewhere legislation is highly discretionary, with requirements of high numbers of students, of specific 'demands' by parents, of subjective standards of literacy, which tend to render the legislation toothless. Foucher remarks that, at least in the Maritime provinces, the guarantees of the *Charter* have been transformed into a group of vague and poorly defined discretionary powers (Foucher, 1985: 33). Monnin confirms that this is the case across the country, and comments on the permissive nature of the language employed in the implementing legislation as well as the reluctance of Anglophone majorities to put any teeth into the procedural provisions. D'Iberville Fortier as well states that constitutional guarantees are most often perceived as discretionary privileges. And as Tarnopolsky points out, one must certainly not allow oneself to be 'hypnotized' by the power of the Constitution. This power and its ability to translate itself into guaranteed rights is only as strong as the will of the people to survive.

Ontario is a key province in the struggle to extend official language minority educational rights due to the fact that it possesses the largest group of French-speaking Canadians outside Quebec. In 1983, it was reported, some 75,000 pupils attended over 300 French-language elementary schools in Ontario and another 32,000 attended the approximately 24 French-language secondary schools or the 36 'mixed' French and English secondary schools (Wardaugh, 1983). Persistent efforts are being made by the Franco-Ontarian community to gain access to their proper share of public monies in the province. What impact

Section 23 will have in this regard will likely be decided by the courts in the context of a highly controversial move by the provincial government to extend public funding through to the final grade of the Catholic (or separate) school system.

> 95% of Ontario's francophones are educated in the separate school system. Virtually all of the parents qualify for publicly funded educational rights under Section 23: they are citizens; they speak French as their maternal language; and the numbers test is obviously satisfied. The separate schools now receive public funding but only to grade ten, and at a vastly inferior rate to that of Anglophone schools in the public system. Under the Charter, however, everyone is entitled to the equal benefit of the law . . . . Over the long term, the Charter may require the complete refining of Ontario's educational system. (Magnet, 1982: 214)

The impact in certain areas of the province will be profound. In some localities entire schools are being transferred from the public to the separate school system. Legislation guaranteeing seats on about 40 school boards is expected, and legislation removing the condition 'where numbers warrant' has been proposed.

Much uncertainty and considerable tension, however, still surround the implementation of official language minority educational rights, and the broader issue of official bilingualism in Ontario and other provinces. In Manitoba the French-language rights issue is particularly volatile, stemming in part from the rejection by Allophones in the Western Provinces of the 'founding peoples' concept of Canada. In New Brunswick, with its French-speaking Acadian population and dual-language-based educational system, tension surrounds a review and planned overhaul of the province's *Official Languages Act* (1969) which made it Canada's only officially bilingual province. And in Quebec, where Anglophones possess their own school boards, the government stresses the crucial importance of other provinces providing French-language institutions, including educational institutions. Quebec, of course, was the only province not to sign the constitutional accord leading to *The Canada Act* (1982) and, in 1989, negotiations are continuing over the Meech Lake Accord for it to add its signature to that of the other provinces.

In addition, in December 1988, Canada's Supreme Court struck down those clauses in Bill 101 pertaining to French-only signs in commercial establishments — a decision the Liberal government of Quebec appeared ready to resist.

Non-official minority language education

The virtual absence of systematic, sociological research on non-official minority, that is, heritage or ancestral, language education in Canada confirms how recently the issue has resurfaced. It also underlines the pressing need to document contemporary developments, if we are to understand the increased demand for this form of education. There is a need, too, to develop conceptual frameworks to help policy-makers and practioners better understand the nature, substance and boundaries of the issue. The concepts and theories articulated in the earlier part of this text are of particular value in this regard.

Adopting a socio-political approach to the analysis of culture, language and schooling — using concepts drawn in large part from critical theory and the 'new sociology of education' — is a case in point. Such an approach provides ways of looking at the public educational system that provides insights into the status of non-official languages (both actual and potential) within the school. It also povides insight into the inherently political nature of conflicts over non-official language education.

These conflicts, are not random, isolated events. They are part of a much broader struggle over the definition of contemporary Canadian society — its culture, institutions and schooling. As the notion of Canada as a monolingual, Anglophone society becomes less and less credible; and as the implementation of bilingual and multicultural policies takes place; the issue of non-official, minority language education takes on added significance. It also provides a window through which to view two contrasting and competing models of Canadian society and culture: dualism and pluralism.

It is highly significant that the *Canadian Charter of Rights and Freedoms* refers to Canada as a multicultural but not a multilingual society. That this is so is hardly surprising, some would even say it is to be expected, given the conflicts over the place and role of the French and English languages in Canada's recent constitutional debates. Nevertheless, as was pointed out earlier, the federal government's policy of 'Multiculturalism within a Bilingual Framework' is replete with contradictions and tensions. Not the least of these involves the status and role of heritage and ancestral languages; and, by extension, what place if any are they to occupy in the curriculum of publicly-funded school systems?

Few systematic analyses of this latter question exist. But some important pointers can be found in a survey conducted by O'Bryan and colleagues titled *The Non-Official Languages Study*. This study, published in 1976, revealed the deep concern of parents in non-official language minority groups over their children's loss of language fluency in heritage languages. It also indicated that these same parents believed the publicly-funded elementary school — not community-based forms of supplementary language training — to be the most appropriate and effective institution to prevent such language loss.

Although the strength of this belief varied among ethno-cultural minority groups (each after all had different experiences, needs and aspirations) the aggregate response was clear. The majority of parents surveyed were not satisfied with their children's proficiency in a language they considered to be an important cultural, social and family asset. Moreover, in an interdependent world economy, fluency in a heritage as well as official languages possessed obvious economic advantages. Why, then, it was asked, could not publicly-funded schools strengthen the language base acquired in the home and community? In the past, languages other than the official languages had been taught in Canadian schools. Why not retrieve and expand upon this tradition whereby which parents, students and teachers could co-operate in a common and mutually reinforcing learning endeavour?

These questions, of course, proved to be much more difficult and complex to answer than to pose. This was due partly to problems associated with the cost and logistics of implementation and partly to the unfamiliarity of non-official language minority groups with how the public school systems operated. However, it was also due to the fact that professional educators and school trustees had certain views as to what constituted acceptable subjects of instruction and what did not. Thus to raise the issue of instruction in heritage or ancestral languages in state-financed educational systems means raising fundamental questions about the purpose of Canadian schooling and by extension the nature of Canadian culture and society.

It is worth recalling why this is the case. Earlier it was demonstrated that culture, language and schooling (as well as the relations between them in Canada) are profoundly political processes. It was pointed out, furthermore, that control over these processes was exercised by the majority and/or dominant group. School systems do not operate autonomously; rather they form an integral part of a larger network of social, political and economic structures and institutions. Similarly, their formally approved curricula do not exist in a vacuum. They are deliberate social constructs, developed by certain groups in a particular time and in a particular setting, aimed at achieving specified outcomes. They represent conscious selections from a larger cultural tradition or traditions.

Schools and school curricula are consciously designed to conserve and transmit certain values, knowledges, skills, competencies, attitudes and patterns of behaviour. They exclude as well as include elements of a society's culture and cultural traditions. Canada, despite its claim to being a plural society, the cultures and languages of the majority (Francophone in Quebec, Anglophone elsewhere) dominate the curricula of the public schools — even in schools where children drawn from non-official language groups form the majority. This is an illustration of how the cultural hegemony of the dominant group is reinforced by schools. Selected aspects of the dominant culture are legitimated and the contribution of minority cultures and languages are marginalized.

If this were all that could be said about the political-sociology of schooling, then one might assume that the aspirations of non-official minority language parents (to have their language represented in the public schools) would likely not be fulfilled.

Culture, language and schooling, however, are not static processes. On the contrary, they are dynamic processes subject to reinforcement, contestation and change. Schools, furthermore, frequently serve as arenas in which the dominant group's hegemony and definition of valued cultural capital (as reflected in the organization and content of the school curricula) are resisted. By demonstrating such resistance, by challenging dominant group interpretations of what should constitute culture and schooling, non-official language groups can achieve several important goals. They can affirm and strengthen their culture, language and identity. They can contribute to the ongoing definition of what constitutes authentic Canadian culture. And they can help determine whether publicly funded institutions and structures are responding appropriately and effectively to its expression.

The efforts of non-official minority language groups to translate their aspirations into programmatic and institutional form in Canada's public school systems are most meaningfully viewed from this perspective. Initially, these efforts resulted in the establishment of experimental programs in which heritage languages were taught as a school subject. Experiments in using heritage languages as languages of instruction followed. In Quebec, for example, certain provincially-aided schools offered trilingual instruction in French, English and Hebrew or Greek (*Equality Now*, 1983). In Alberta, Saskatchewan and the Northwest Territories legislation was introduced to permit the use of heritage languages as a medium as well as a subject of instruction. And bilingual English–Ukrainian and English–German programs were established in Alberta, Manitoba and Saskatchewan (Mallea, 1984a).

Space does not permit analysis of each and every one of these examples. The importance of context, however, underlines the importance of illustrating developments in non-official minority language education in more concrete fashion. Two case-studies, therefore are presented. Drawn from two different cities and provinces, they vividly reveal not only the political nature of educational decision-making but also the interconnectedness of Canadian educational policy at the national, provincial and municipal levels. They also illustrate how differences in approach, process and outcome are shaped by political, historical and demographic factors.

Edmonton, Alberta

The first of the two case-studies involves the successful introduction of a bilingual English–Ukrainian program in the public and separate school systems in Edmonton, Alberta. It provides an excellent example of sophisticated, special-interest group politics resulting in an amendment to the *Alberta School Act* and the allocation of public funds in support of a non-official minority language in the curriculum of both public and separate (Catholic) school boards.

In December 1970, the Ukrainian Professional and Businessman's Club (UKPBC) established a committee to prepare a brief to the Government of Alberta subsequently titled 'The Ukrainians, the New Canadian Constitution, the Laws of Alberta and the Policies of the Government of Alberta'.[1] On April 14, 1971, a delegation from the UKPBC, accompanied by the President of the Ukrainian Canadian Committee, held a meeting with the Premier of Alberta, the Minister of Education, the Attorney General, and the Minister of Culture, Youth and Recreation to discuss its concerns. What transpired at the meeting is not generally known. But within two weeks an amendment to the *Alberta School Act* was approved that stated: 'A board may authorize that any other language be used as the language of instruction in addition to the English language, in all or any of its schools' (Lupul & Savaryn, 1974). The use of Ukrainian as a language of instruction in the public schools of Alberta was not only possible — it was legitimated in law. Preparations were now set in train to translate permissive legislation into reality.

The UKPBC immediately made an approach to Edmonton's two school boards seeking to discuss the introduction of English–Ukrainian bilingual programs. 50% of instruction in the school curriculum was to be given in English and 50% in Ukrainian.[2] Before they could be introduced, however, a provincial election was held (in the summer of 1971) which resulted in a major political upset and a change in government. The UKPBC multiculturalism committee turned its attention to the task of establishing political relationships with the new government. A year and a half later, in March 1973, a dinner meeting was arranged with the Minister of Education, the Minister of Advanced Education and the Minister of Manpower and Labour during which a three-year pilot project was discussed. The outcome of the discussion proved disappointing. Hence Edmonton's Ukrainian community brought additional pressure to bear by launching a public criticism of the government's cultural policy — a policy it declared was only a 'facade'.

Stung by this criticism, and the coverage it received in the news media, the Minister of Culture, Youth and Recreation attempted to defend the government's policy but to no avail. As his critics pointed out, aid to language instruction — the Ukrainian community's 'greatest need' — was not being provided. At this point, the government obviously reconsidered its position and shortly thereafter the Minister of Education funded the three-year pilot project that had been the subject of earlier discussions.

The Ukrainian–Canadian community and particularly the UKPBC's Multiculturalism Committee now swung into action. The Multiculturalism Committee arranged separate meetings with the Minister of Education, the Superintendent of Education of the Edmonton Public School Board and the Superintendent of Education of the Edmonton Separate School Board. A meeting was held also with the Associate Deputy Minister of Education attended by the provincial Department of Education's Director of Curriculum, the Associate Director of Curriculum (Languages), the Supervisor of Second Languages in the Edmonton Public School Board, the Superintendent and Deputy Superintendent of the Edmonton Separate School Board, and three members of the UKPBC's Multiculturalism Committee.

Negotiations among these parties resulted in an agreement in February 1974. The Department of Education agreed to commit $50,000 per year for three years to hire a Ukrainian curriculum specialist, prepare appropriate curriculum materials, pay for two half-time consultants (one each for the public and separate school systems), and meet transportation costs according to existing regulations. As an additional cost, the Department would also pay 80% of the amount needed to evaluate the program at appropriate times. For its part, the Ukrainian community agreed to guarantee no fewer than 100 students in Grade 1 (Lupul & Savaryn, 1974).

The three-year pilot project was launched in the same year that the agreement was reached. Subsequently, several formal evaluations have been conducted which have demonstrated its viability and worth. The program has also grown to extend from kindergarten through grade 11 (Jones & Miedem, 1984; Mallea, 1984a). Indeed, it shows every sign of becoming a permanent feature of the educational system in Alberta. And, what is of equal importance, perhaps, the program has served as an example to other non-official language minority communities in the neighbouring Western provinces as well as attracting the attention of groups in Central and Eastern Canada.

Toronto, Ontario

The second of the two case-studies to be presented involves the introduction of non-official minority language instruction (or heritage languages) into the City of Toronto Board of Education's schools. Here the issue had been the subject of continuing controversy from the mid-1970s on (Cummins, 1984). During these years, a number of ethno-cultural groups campaigned vigorously for the inclusion of heritage languages as a subject of instruction in the regular school curriculum. Others, drawn mainly, but not exclusively, from the Anglophone majority, vigorously opposed it. The issue assumed a high profile and divided communities, parents, teachers and elected school board trustees. It attracted considerable attention from the media, teacher associations, other school boards, various municipal governments, the provincial Ministry of Education and the federal government.

A brief historical overview of the issue helps explain why it attracted so much attention and caused so much controversy on all sides. Since the early 1970s several heritage-language programs had existed in the City of Toronto schools. These were essentially experimental projects which, while popular and successful attracted little attention.

Then, in the mid 1970s, the Board of Education established a Task Force on Multiculturalism which actively solicited briefs from interested parties. Even a cursory glance at the contents of the briefs received reveals just how sharp a division of belief existed on the role of the public school in helping maintain and enhance fluency in the city's many heritage languages. On the whole, briefs from minority ethnocultural groups stressed the important role the public school had to play, while those submitted by professional educators placed much greater emphasis on the role of group and community organizations (Masemann, 1978–79). This serious division of opinion could not be ignored by the Task Force whose initial report titled 'The Bias of Culture' (1975) addressed the matter directly. Nevertheless, its final report, although generally supportive, did not recommend the inclusion of instruction in heritage languages in the regular school day (Final Report, 1976).

Undaunted, ethnocultural minority groups, whose children numbered over 50% of those enrolled in the City of Toronto's public schools, continued to press for greater recognition for their languages. They resisted attempts to sideline or defuse the issue. They lobbied continually to achieve the inclusion of heritage languages in the regular school day. In brief, they argued they wanted a school curriculum that more accurately reflected contemporary demographic realities and which not only recognized but validated their cultures and languages.

Efforts toward this end continued and, by dint of skilful lobbying, plus the support of a few elected school trustees and sympathetic school administrators, they were rewarded. In 1980, the Board of Education established a Work Group on Heritage Languages made up of trustees, community representatives, administrators and teachers. Its mandate: to examine the place of heritage languages in the public school system. The Work Group solicited briefs, held public meetings across the city, and listened to presentations from both a wide range of lay and professional groups. Eighteen months later it produced a report 'Towards a Comprehensive Language Policy' which recommended the inclusion of heritage languages in the regular school day of a selected number of schools.

This report was subsequently placed before the Board of Education for discussion and vote. Recognizing the controversial nature of the Work Group's main recommendation, the Board of Education scheduled a lengthy meeting to extend over several evenings. In the event, this proved appropriate. More than 200 individuals, groups and expert witnesses made presentations. Hundreds of people, many carrying placards for and against heritage languages, made up a passioniately involved, overflow audience. Many representatives of the local print and electronic media were in attendance and the stage was set for what proved to be a prolonged and acrimonious exchange of views.

The substance and tone of this exchange illustrated very well the utility of employing a socio-political approach to the analysis of culture, language and schooling. It also underlined the dynamic, dialectical nature of the policy formation and decision-making process in the field of publicly funded education. Many of the presenters expressed views resting on a variety of conflicting assumptions about what did and should constitute Canadian society and its institutions. Three broad patterns of thought and belief stood out. Some, for example, expressed the view that both Ontario and Canada represented an established monocultural, unilingual Anglophone community and that minority ethnic groups should assimilate to this model. Schools, moreover, should aid in this assimilation with English being the sole language of instruction. Others took the position that the British and the French were Canada's two founding or charter groups and English and French should be the languages of instruction (a position supported by the *Ontario Education Act*). Still others, supported the federal government's policy of 'Multiculturalism within a Bilingual Framework' but were not prepared to support the concept of a multilingual education.

Those that supported the teaching of heritage languages during the regular school day resisted all three of the above positions and argued strongly that Canadian society was a culturally and linguistically plural society and that this fact should be reflected in its educational instructions. Pointing to the demographic, linguistic, racial and cultural realities of Toronto, they vigorously represented the view that the city was a multilingual community. It was entirely appropriate, therefore, in their view, that tax-supported public schools should build on the dynamism of this evolving community and reap its benefits: pedagogical, social, and economic) Children's knowledge of heritage languages, they proposed, fostered a positive sense of their identity, promoted inter-generational communication, contributed to social cohesion, and facilitated access to other cultures.

Given the above assumptions about Canadian society and the role of its public school system, it will come as no surprise to learn that there was no consensus among the Board of Education trustees as to what policy on heritage languages they should adopt. Passions were aroused, strong words were spoken and it soon became clear that the vote would be close. This proved to be the case. When the vote was taken the recommendation of the Work Group on Heritage Languages that instruction in them be included in the regular school day, passed by the narrowest of margins. That it did so was due in very large part to the fact that the informal New Democratic Party caucus on the Board threw its support behind the recommendation. Politics, this time partisan party politics, for the New Democrats formed one of the two opposition parties in the province, had once again proved to be a decisive factor in the making of educational policy.

The making of policy is one thing, but its implementation is quite another matter altogether. In this case, the furore over the proposed implementation of the policy once again confirmed the contested relationship of Canadian culture, language and schooling. What occurred is instructive.

While the City of Toronto School Trustees were debating heritage languages, the Progressive Conservative Government's Ministry of Education, expressing concern about the quality of learning in core subjects such as English and science (the use of the word 'core' is also instructive) extended the public elementary school day by half an hour. In effect, this meant that if instruction in heritage languages were to be incorporated into the school day, then it would have to be extended by one full hour. Suspicions were quickly voiced that the timing of the provincial government's decision was not coincidental. It was not these charges, however, but the actions of the professional associations of teachers and principals, that fueled the next phase of the conflict.

The membership of the Toronto Teachers Federation (TTF) and the Toronto Public Schools Principals Association (TPSPA), despite their representatives on the implementation committee being supportive, expressed a number of serious reservations about the proposed integration of heritage language instruction into the regular school day. Two concerns appeared paramount, however. The impact of integration on the scheduling of extra-curricular activities and changes in the allocation of scarce resources resulting from its introduction. Feelings on these issues were strong. Discussion proved fruitless. Claims and counter claims were made. And at the annual meeting of the Toronto Teachers Federation, shortly after implementation of the integration policy began, the membership elected a new executive to oppose integration. Subsequently, the new executive, during their collective bargaining negotiations with the Board, made the issue a condition of agreement for a new contract. The Board refused and the entire matter was submitted for formal arbitration.

Subsequently a three-person panel was appointed to arbitrate the issue of the 'integration of current Heritage Language Classes with the regular school day'. It did so, and by a vote of two to one, the panel rejected the teachers' association proposition that Heritage Language programs be excluded from the regular teaching day. The place of non-official language instruction in the school curriculum in the City of Toronto's schools was declared legitimate and implementation of the program continued.

The meaning of the above controversy is clear. It reinforces the general point made earlier in the text: namely, that the controversy is not so much about heritage languages as it is about the nature of Canadian society and the type of schooling it is prepared to support from public funds. Nor is the issue resolved. Rather it has moved to a larger arena of debate: the provincial legislature. In early 1987, a private members bill (Bill 80) was introduced by a member of the New Democratic Party, an opposition party which had entered into an agreement with the governing Liberal party, proposing that a heritage language class should be established in any public or separate school of Ontario if twenty or more students (or their parents) requested it. The Bill was in second reading, and public hearings on it were being held when a provincial election was called.

The election resulted in a landslide victory for the Liberals. Subsequently, in 1988 heritage language legislation was introduced and passed making it mandatory for schools to offer heritage language instruction where requested and where the appropriate numbers to form a class were in place.

Conclusion

The primary aim of this chapter was to provide examples of major areas of ongoing conflict over schooling. A second aim was to throw into bold relief the limitations of oversimplified versions of existing monocultural, bicultural and multicultural models in contemporary Canadian society. Issues of governance, funding, institutional forms and curricular content were addressed and alternative models, forms and structures described.

The issue of aboriginal rights raises fundamental questions about the meaning of democratic pluralism in Canada: What right does a racial, cultural, linguistic and ethnic majority group have to exist as a distinct collective within the political system? What rights do such groups have to protect their collective identities? What forms of participation are guaranteed in our legal, economic, political, social and public educational systems to ensure that these rights can be exercised? What institutions and structures, especially in the area of publicly-funded education, might best reflect the expression of these democratic rights in a dual and plural Canada?

Answers to these and related questions have been far from encouraging to date. Neither the assimilationist model of Canadian majority–minority relations, the dualist or bilingual–bicultural model, nor the hybrid multicultural–bilingual model, has resulted in support for the continuance of native cultures. The current unequal distribution of economic and political powers, buttressed by white-dominated legal structures and social institutions, have further marginalized aboriginal cultures, languages and identities. Publicly-funded educational systems have reinforced this process by placing little or no value on the cultural capital native students bring to school.

As the historical record reveals, aboriginal peoples have repeatedly resisted such deficit theories of cultural capital, vigorously opposed racially-biased models of schooling, and repeatedly drawn attention to the contradictions they contain. Today, aboriginal peoples are systematically contesting the authenticity and legitimacy of current forms of public schooling, and the conventional models of Canadian dualism and pluralism from which they derive. Their collective rights in this regard are receiving much greater recognition; new forms of governance are being introduced; and innovative educational structures are being established. New institutional forms are being developed, and differentiated school curricula and hiring patterns can be observed.

These efforts at resolving the contradictions and tensions of Canadian dualism and pluralism are not restricted to questions of aboriginal rights. As we have seen, they are also central to the political, legal and constitutional struggles of official and non-official language groups.

The most striking aspect of current efforts to resolve the tensions surrounding the provision (or lack of provision) of official language minority education is the degree to which the *Canadian Charter of Rights and Freedoms* (1982) is being invoked. The official language minority educational rights section of the Charter underlines, as few other things can, the abiding centrality of language and education in the Canadian context. Both, as we have seen, are inextricably linked to the larger political, economic and cultural sectors.

Passage of the *Canadian Charter of Rights and Freedoms* (1982) gave renewed hope to official language minority groups throughout the country. And, as the preceding pages reveal, in certain provinces and regions these groups are seeking structural as well as institutional and curricular changes. Governance issues are at the heart of efforts to bring about legislative change and further court challenges are expected. On the constitutional front, meanwhile, Quebec is prepared to sign a proposed constitutional agreement which recognizes it as a 'distinct society'. Whether the proposed Meech Lake accord will be translated into law, however, remains a disputed point with several provinces debating whether or not to add their signature to it.

On a brighter note, research on these matters in a variety of locales and settings is becoming more extensive. One can now turn to an expanding research literature on native governance issues and official language minority education. This is less the case, however, with respect to research on non-official or heritage languages education. It is therefore worth identifying in greater detail, promising lines of future research on this issue.

Enough has been said, in the above section on heritage language education to suggest that the application of the earlier theoretical discussion is suggestive of rich possibilities. For example, adoption of a theoretical approach which emphasizes the political sociology of culture and schooling, and its related concepts and frameworks, could help us understand more clearly attempts by minority groups to introduce heritage language instruction into the regular school curriculum. Its application in different settings, moreover, would dramatize the differences that can and do exist between these attempts in a society that is as heterogeneous and decentralized as Canada. Enough, too, has probably been said on this issue to reinforce the central fact that culture, language and schooling are vigorously contested areas of life in which heritage language groups continue to resist dominant group interpretations of what constitutes Canadian culture and authentic school content. The struggles which result also serve to reinforce the fact that the provincial and territorial educational systems are embedded in much wider and interlocking systems of economic, political and cultural structures and institutions. Their relationships, moreover, are not static. Rather, as we have seen, they are dynamic and hence possess potentiality for change.

A second point to be made about the links between sociological theory and research on heritage languages is that the need exists to employ a variety of analytical approaches. To date, in much of the literature on schooling in plural societies, notions of cultural pluralism has assumed pride of place. More often than not, too, they have been employed without benefit of definition or demonstrated links to other forms of pluralism. In the case of normative pluralism, for example, of which Canadian federal and provincial policies of multiculturalism are good illustrations, few attempts have been made to relate cultural pluralism to political, structural and institutional forms of pluralism. There is much to be gained from doing so, however. For example, much of the current efforts of ethnocultural minority groups are aimed at obtaining institutional and structural expression of their aspirations — especially in the area of language.

A third area in which there is a pressing need for sociological research, employing the concepts and theories described in this text, is within the schools themselves. What are the day-to-day realities, the lived experience of students and staff, in schools where heritage language programs are operating? What types of programs exist, who enrols in them, from which groups and which socio-economic strata? How well are students achieving in these programs? Who are the teachers and what are their qualifications? How are they viewed by their colleagues? What perceptions do the latter have of heritage language policies, programs and their implementation? How does it affect their schedules and working conditions? What positions have teachers' organizations adopted in the matter and how are they being expressed? In addition, similar questions can be asked regarding communities and their organizations.

A fourth approach that holds promise of illuminating heritage language issues is the comparative approach. In a multiracial, multicultural society, there are good reasons for making inter-regional, inter-provincial, inter-city, inter-group and inter-institutional comparisons. Within as well as between group comparisons are also to be recommended. The similarities and differences that exist, and which this type of research would reveal, could provide valuable specificity as well as insights into the forces and factors that determine contemporary provision for heritage languages in Canadian schools.

The fifth area in which research is needed deals with the impact of research on heritage languages on public policy making. To what extent do interest groups and decision makers at all levels make use of existing research findings and to what ends? What impact, for example, have the findings of studies of non-official languages majority attitudes study had on decisions regarding heritage language programs? Do these research findings have little direct influence on specific policy decisions? Or do they exert their influence more by way of affecting the manner in which these decisions are reached and acted upon?

Such questions, and the absence of answers to them, confirm the urgent need for research. Until such research is conducted, interest groups and public policymakers will lack a key ingredient in the decision-making process. And schools will continue to serve as arenas of struggle and conflict and social cohesion and national integration will be hindered.

Schools though, are only a part of a larger whole. If social cohesion and national integration are to be meaningful to many citizens with non-British and non-French backgrounds, then the nation's economic, political and social institutions will have to encourage their greater participation. Concrete recognition by Canadian public school systems of the curricular legitimacy of heritage cultures and languages, and appreciation of how they might help promote a more authentic Canadian culture, may well be one of the best places to begin.

Notes to Chapter 5

1 The information that follows is drawn from a little known article by Lupul & Savaryn (1974).
2 An excellent description and evaluation of these programs can be found elsewhere (see, for example, Lamont et al., 1978).

6 Summary and conclusions

The aim of this brief text has been to examine the relationship between schooling and pluralism in Canada by way of relevant theory. In pursuing this aim, the limitations of traditional theories of both schooling and pluralism have been revealed and alternative theories and approaches advanced. What contribution these alternatives will make to our understanding largely remains a question for the future. Yet sufficient discussion has taken place to indicate they possess greater value than earlier theoretical attempts at explanation.

This summary and concluding chapter brings the text to a close by reviewing the utility of these alternatives in the Canadian context. A precise summary of each is not attempted, rather the chapter focuses on their complementary aspects and their combined force. In brief, when combined, they are suggestive of a more comprehensive theory of schooling that takes directly into account the racial, cultural and linguistic diversity of a plural Canada.

Three broad and competing models currently exist about what constitutes or should constitute authentic contemporary Canadian culture: monoculturalism, biculturalism and multiculturalism. Monoculturalism stresses uniformity and finds expression in both anglo-conformity and franco-conformity; biculturalism is rooted firmly in the concept of English–French duality; and multiculturalism emphasizes broader notions of pluralism.

Each model, it has been argued, has its supporters and a more or less well-defined ideology and matrix of ideas, images and concepts. Each is associated with one of three positions on language: unilingualism, bilingualism and multilingualism. Each influences the positions taken by majority and minority groups on issues involving the politics of Canadian culture. And each has exerted considerable influence over the goals, governance, content and conduct of publicly funded schooling.

The existence of these competing versions of what constitutes the legitimate Canadian cultural model has resulted inevitably in tensions, struggles and conflicts. At different times, and in different settings, linguistic strife, racial tensions and religious struggles have formed major leitmotifs in the history of Canadian politics, culture, and schooling. Not surprisingly, the educational ideologies associated with conformist, dualistic and pluralistic concepts of Canada have varied over time and from location to location. Each has affected the other and has been affected in turn. The process of schooling is a dynamic one and, like the processes of culture and inter-group relations is continuously produced, reproduced and resisted. It contributes significantly to the maintenance, development and resolution of existing ambiguities, contradictions and tensions on a societal level.

Resolution of these tensions is made difficult by the existence of competing centripetal and centrifugal forces in plural societies. All societies, of course, require elements of centripetality if they are to function effectively, but plural societies clearly have to learn to live with greater measures of centrifugality than their more homogeneous counterparts. This fact has major implications for public educational systems which are frequently designated the major formal agency by which selected values, attitudes, skills and knowledge are transmitted from one generation to the next. In Canada, as elsewhere, the responsibility for their selection has rested largely in the hands of dominant cultural groups functioning as guardians and sustainers of controlling value systems and the prime allocators of rewards.

It was in an effort to reduce inter-group tensions, it will be recalled, that the policy of *Multiculturalism Within a Bilingual Framework* was approved by parliament in 1971. This policy firmly rejected the monocultural and bicultural models of Canadian society declaring them undesirable and unacceptable goals for Canada. There were two official languages; but there was no official culture and no ethnic group was to take precedence over any other — all citizens were Canadians and all were to be treated fairly.

It will also be recalled that the federal government's policy of *Multiculturalism Within a Bilingual Framework* expresses support for the preservation of basic human rights, the elimination of discrimination, the encouragement of cultural diversity, the strengthening of citizen participation, and the reinforcement of Canadian identity. Its aim is to help create a sense of identity, belonging, and individual freedom of choice which in turn are to form the basis of national unity. Ethnic loyalties, the policy emphasizes, need not and indeed usually does not, detract from wider loyalties to community and country.

From the introduction of the federal policy, analysts of multicultural education, have adopted markedly different interpretations of its intent. Some viewed it as a sincere effort to alter the vertical mosaic through a process of attitude change. Others consider that it seeks to legitimize the *status quo*. Still others point to the gross imbalances of power among different ethnic groups, criticize the isolation of culture and education from economic realities, and underline the low priority implementation of multicultural education has received. There are those, too, who are sceptical that the idealized goal of cultural harmony (which underlies most multicultural education policies and programs) will result in any reduction of existing inequalities.

For their part, social scientists have criticized the lack of conceptual clarity surrounding multiculturalism and multicultural education, considered their intellectual foundations to be shaky, and have stressed the need for more systematic, scholarly analyses: Are multiculturalism and multicultural education socio-political instruments for ensuring cooperation by the granting of limited concessions? Are they designed to realize democratic ideals or are they another form of social control? Do multicultural education policies assume knowledge will reduce prejudice and discrimination? Do they recognize and legitimize cultural differences while failing to deal with racism at the institutional, structural and individual level? Or as some argue, do current approaches help maintain the myth about subordinate groups as 'problems to be studied', while leaving institutional and structural inequalities intact? Is the cultural capital minority children bring to school seen as different but valid, or inappropriate and deficient? Are multicultural programs and materials included for educational or therapeutic purposes? Do they celebrate individual social mobility but ignore ethnic stratification? Do they stress consensus while trying to ignore or avoid conflicts?

Answers to these questions lie at the heart of what we have termed the pluralist dilemma in Canadian education — a dilemma which arises out of the need to balance the educational needs and aspirations of minority and majority groups. Schools, for instance, are expected to embrace cultural diversity while promoting overarching goals of social cohesion and national integration. Admittedly, this task has never been an easy one. And it is rendered even more difficult by the absence of any clearly formulated national policies of education.

Increasingly policy-makers have looked to scholars in the social sciences for help in responding to the pluralist dilemma in education but such assistance is not always available. One major reason for this is that analyses of schooling, and in particular multicultural education, have not been well grounded in these disciplines. Why this is so is not entirely clear. On the other hand, as we have seen, there are at least five identifiable reasons why traditional theory has offered only limited aid.

First, it was observed that the dialectic between the universal and particular cannot be resolved by appeal to any all-encompassing set of principles but must be worked out generation by generation in the context of the day. Second, plural societies are characterized by the co-existence of autonomous but non-complementary sub-societies; hence, what coherence exists cannot be fully accounted for by value consensus. Third, existing theories of pluralism lack a theory of power and fail to examine power relations, decision-making, and policy formulation in terms of the broader societal structure of power; and, in particular, they fail to address power differentials and the ordering of power relations in the structuring of state-aided public education. Fourth, they frequently ignore the tensions between political democracy and economic inequality. And, fifth, they rarely analyse schooling except in terms of the very limited context of cultural differences. Consequently, no comprehensive theories of Canadian pluralism and schooling have been developed.

In addition, prevailing liberal and conservative perspectives of schooling, and the assumptions on which they rest, are rarely the subject of in-depth scrutiny and appraisal. The theoretical literature on race and ethnic relations rarely contains systematic analyses of schooling. The explanatory power of existing classificatory systems is limited and seriously underestimates the contested nature of race and ethnic relations in education. What studies have been carried out, moreover, are almost entirely conducted from the viewpoint of the dominant group, while studies undertaken from the point of view of subordinate groups are virtually non-existent.

Rarely, indeed, have conflicts over schooling in a plural Canada been systematically examined in socio-economic, political, institutional and structural terms. Prevailing theories have stressed instead the school's role in cultural transmission and emphasized notions of neutrality, stability and consensus. Priority is given to this role and educational institutions and structures have been established whose primary function is the maintenance of existing systems. Whether they are good or bad in terms of individual preferences or ethnocultural group aspirations has been considered less important.

Limitations such as these have given rise among social scientists to a search for more fruitful lines of enquiry which recognize the explanatory potential of power-conflict theory. Conflicts over schooling require the application of power to attain and maintain control, and efforts to resolve them lead to the development of unequal power relations and continuing struggles for control. Emphasis, therefore, is placed on change rather than preservation of the *status quo*.

In Canada power-conflict theory has been seen as a valuable corrective to structural-functional analyses of society and education. It has demonstrated convincingly that Canadian society is stratified and that for some groups public education does not lead to upward social mobility. By relating existing institutions and structures to class or status group interests, moreover, it has provided a more meaningful and realistic analysis of Canadian society. Nevertheless, power-conflict theory (as is also the case with theories of structural-functionalism) is limited in its analysis of race and ethnicity in education.

Much is to be gained by integrating the structural-functionalist with the power-conflict approach in analyzing schooling in a plural society. At least three mutually reinforcing advantages, it has been argued, can be obtained by adopting this dialectical position. First, the analyst is kept face to face with the concrete realities of social situations, their fluidity and complexity. Second, its adoption does not assume any particular ideological position. And, third, an important analytical distinction is made between culture and structure, which in turn emphasizes the intimate relationship that exists between culture and politics and reveals the interlocking role of symbols (e.g. the language of instruction) and power.

This distinction between culture and structure also underlines the importance of the differences that exist between cultural, normative, political, and socio-economic forms of pluralism. In brief, cultural pluralism refers to the presence of racial and ethnic groups possessing languages and/or other cultural norms and values differentiating them from dominant groups. It is the form of pluralism most often invoked in connection with schooling. Normative or ideological pluralism is usually discussed in terms of the toleration or appreciation of cultural differences. Political pluralism, refers to the existence of a multiplicity of autonomous groups and associations (including but not restricted to those possessing an ethno-cultural base) that exert pressure on the initiation, formulation, and implementation of public policy. Structural pluralism involves the presence of institutions and structures, which may range from a situation where complete duplication of services is provided to a situation where racial and ethnic groups participate in a number of common institutions. And socio-economic pluralism points to the existence of socio-economic stratification along racial, ethnic and linguistic lines. All five, it has been argued, are crucially important in the analysis of schooling in a plural Canada.

Cultural pluralism, while rarely defined and often employed loosely in the literature on multicultural education, is of value in describing objective cultural differences. Normative or ideological pluralism is important because the ideological system shapes, structures and coordinates all other cultural and social systems. Hence, for example, in Canada, normative ideals of pluralism serve as important sources of cohesion and unity. Such ideals can and should be subjected to critical scrutiny — especially in the field of education whose role in the stablization of ideological systems is widely acknowledged.

Institutional and structural pluralism are valuable concepts that not only help document the existence of plural institutions and structures but also reinforce the differing degrees of power, wealth and knowledge possessed by dominant and subordinate ethnic groups. They help us understand the institutionalized relationships which exist within and help maintain Canada's social, political and economic structures. They illustrate the control over these structures exercised by dominant groups. They demonstrate how the status of a subordinate group's culture is related directly to that group's position in the economic and political structure. And, they are of considerable value in analyzing how educational institutions and structures select, reproduce and legitimize different forms of cultural capital.

Political pluralism, employed as an analytical concept, helps us understand the processes whereby a multiplicity of autonomous groups and associations (including those possessing a racial and ethnocultural base) bring pressure to bear on the development and implementation of political decisions. It can help explain, for example, why ethnic politics are so attractive and why ethnicity is such a potent basis of political mobilization and action. More importantly, however, it can help reverse the traditional approach of political scientists to the analysis of public education in Canada. As argued above, political scientists in Canada have largely confined their analyses to the study of educational policy. In doing so they have consciously or unconsciously replaced political questions with questions of educational decision-making and administration. As a result, research on ethnicity and education has largely conceived of politics and school systems as intersecting at one point: the socialization of ethnic minorities to the dominant culture. Ethnicity has been seen as a categorical reference point rather than a process and ethnic groups have been treated as static systems which constrain the political integration of the nation.

A similar form of reductionism has been practiced with respect to socio-economic pluralism. No one questions the fact that social and ethnic stratification exists in Canada and that socio-economic differences are one of the most important forms of differentiation affecting individuals and groups in racially and ethnically plural societies. Yet no general theory of ethnic stratification exists and the resulting tendency to subsume or equate racial and ethnic stratification systems within social stratification blurs the character of these forms of differentiation. This tendency also underestimates the very real disparities in power among racial and ethnic groups and downplays the significance of racism and ethnocentrism. Ethnicity in fact may yet prove to be as important a variable as social class in determining educational outcomes and, thereby helping one determine one's eventual position in the socio-economic hierarchy.

The research literature on ethnicity and educational achievement in Canada, however, is recent, localized and incomplete. Nevertheless the research that has been done suggests a less clear-cut set of relationships than has been argued to date. For example, recent research on educational achievement which distinguishes between specific ethnic groups throws new light on the findings of macro-sociological research. The relative value placed on formal education appears to vary among ethnicities; and each ethnic group seems to be characterized by a unique set of internal social values and relations influencing the functions of formal education within that group.

One can express, therefore, only the most tentative conclusions on group specific relationships between educational attainment, ethnic and social stratification. Consequently, we must broaden our search for explanatory theory in a variety of ways. First, more macro-sociological research is needed if we are to more fully appreciate the structural relations between educational systems and the economy. Second, and perhaps more importantly, increased attention needs to be given to micro-sociological studies so as to understand better the links between these structures and the internal processes of the school. Most importantly of all, however, we must systematically integrate these two types of research. Structure and process are inextricably joined and schools form part of a much larger, interlocking patterns of institutions, structures and processes (political, economic, social and cultural). The school's relationships to the broader political and economic system are further informed by a complex set of differential power relations which results in the dominant racial, cultural and linguistic groups in Canada exercising control over the governance, administration, curricula and practices of publicly funded school systems.

Exercise of this control, it has been argued, has resulted in a series of conscious selections being made whereby the knowledge, contents, skills and values of Canada's hegemonic groups have dominated. The hierarchical structure and organization of curricula clearly reflects these judgements and the different allocations of time, resources and status accorded various subjects of study confirm them. So, too, does the treatment accorded the curricular content advanced by subordinate ethnocultural groups. For the most part, these have been treated as either supplementary activities or excluded altogether.

Seeking further explanation of these realities confirmed the importance of adding contributions drawn from theories of culture to the dialectical analysis approach resulting from the integration of structural-functionalism and power-conflict theories. Theories of culture have historically found their basis in one or the other of three ideological traditions: conservative, liberal-democratic or Marxist. The first assumes that culture is largely static and to be conserved; the second that the individual, (and individual expression), is the key element in the production of culture; and the third, that the economic structure is of central importance in its formation. All three traditions consider culture to be a central concept in any comprehensive theory of society and all three believe schooling plays a central role in its transmission.

Of late, however, these traditional explanations of culture and schooling have come under considerable criticism. In particular, the necessity to rethink the linkages between culture, economic and political power — especially the power of dominant groups to reproduce their culture in the school — has been stressed.

By viewing culture as a valuable resource (cultural capital) the control over the form and content of which is contested, we can better understand current conflicts over schooling. As is well known, the question of which specific knowledge, belief systems and values are to be transmitted by schools is problematic. Nor is it simply a question of what culture and what heritage to transmit. Whose culture and whose heritage is also at issue. The fact that certain types of school knowledge are more highly rated than others is not in doubt. Why this is so, why such hierarchies exist, is much less clear.

The concept of cultural capital, when linked with the concept of cultural hegemony, strongly suggests that this process of selection and hierarchical ordering is largely determined by the power of the dominant culture group. Language is a clear case in point. With very few exceptions, the language of instruction in a community is the language of the dominant or majority group. And schools further reinforce the importance of this language in mediating relationships between dominant and subordinate groups. That is, they help produce, reproduce and legitimate differential relations among majority and minority, racial and ethnocultural groups.

Advocates of reproduction theory, for example, have rejected any notion of the educational system as a closed and neutral system. On the contrary, they view education as a permeable system, one deeply affected by the cultural and socio-economic resources children bring to the school. From their perspective, school success is the result of an unequal contest in which all children do not receive equal treatment or exposure to the same formal culture irrespective of background. It is better explained by the school's reproduction of the culture of the dominant group. This process, moreover, is intimately connected to a larger process whereby the social, economic and political characteristics of a group are reproduced. It is also inseparably connected to the reproduction of relations between dominant and subordinate racial, ethnic and linguistic groups. This results from direct and indirect applications of power by the dominant group. Mainstream culture is largely determined by these relations and is compatible with the cultural tradition of the dominant group.

Cultural legitimation, a concept closely linked to that of cultural reproduction, further suggests that claims of legitimacy for school curricula and practices are largely derived from the authority and power possessed by the dominant cultural group. That is, schools and school curricula not only transmit and distribute the cultural capital of the dominant group, they legitimize it by investing it with qualities of objectivity, neutrality, and even universality. Such conferral of legitimacy cannot be taken for granted, however. For, as we have seen, the arbitrary imposition of knowledge and culture is resisted frequently by minority groups.

Such cultural resistance is an active process. It is a political act involving actors, processes and structures internal and external to the educational system. It directs attention to the ways in which racial and ethnic minorities attempt to make schools responsive to the transmission of their cultures. And it underlines the fact that the process of cultural legitimation must be reworked as conditions and inter-group relations undergo modification and change.

This process, moreover, can best be understood by employing concepts such as cultural hegemony which reveal that the selection and hierarchical ordering of curricula are largely determined by dominant groups. School curricula reflect their preferred knowledge content, cultural values and traditions. Such exercise of power, however, the imposition by the dominant group(s) of a specific cultural design, based on its possession of power, is neither fixed nor unchanging. It has to be renewed continually in the context of resistance by subordinate (racial, cultural and linguistic) groups.

It is also important to realize that the theories and concepts outlined in this text possess combined as well as individual force. Employed in aggregate and complementary ways, they are suggestive of a more comprehensive theory of schooling that takes into account the realities of racial, cultural and linguistic pluralism. This is because they offer a more relational than functional analysis of schooling, and, while employing a more conflict- than system-oriented approach, they also value some types of structural analysis. By emphasizing the power dimensions of inter-group relations, they underline the importance of the exercise of power in determining the characteristic forms and outcomes of public schooling. Much of their persuasiveness is lodged in the explicit recognition that the processes of culture and schooling are inherently political. And, by recognizing the ways in which historical background influences current conditions, they provide a larger framework within which the specific findings can be placed.

The combining of these theories also provides a valuable counterpoint to the overly tight conceptual fit between schooling and reproduction in the work of some theorists. The metaphor of reproduction can be pushed too far and when this occurs it obscures the processes of relative autonomy and change within school and school systems. The same is true with respect to the school system's relationships to other systems. Moreover, the approach advocated here accords a more influential place to cultural (as opposed to social) reproduction and reinforces the need to analyse the cultural production and reproduction of subordinate groups in analyses of schooling in a plural society.

Theories of resistance perform a particularly valuable service in this regard. By rejecting the idea that schools are merely instructional sites, they help politicize the concept of culture, locate the culture of the school firmly within a contested realm, and underline the importance of lived experiences. They also reinforce the fact that what goes on in schools and school classrooms are the products of dynamic, historical forces. That is, patterns of classroom relations, forms of authority, belief systems and languages of instruction are concrete outcomes of contested relationships between dominant and subordinate groups.

It is essential, therefore, to ground studies of Canadian schooling firmly within their context. They could explore, for example, linkages between cultural deficit theory and prevailing forms of cultural capital. The unilateral adaption of minority cultures to that of the majority inherent in policies of compensatory education suggests another area of study. The practice of labelling illustrates how narrowly conceived notions of cultural capital can result in 'blaming the victim', rather than the system which generates conditions of failure. Even when analysts have focused on the dysfunctional aspects of schooling, they have neglected to explain why schools seem to work to the advantage of certain groups and not others. Their explanations have not been pursued in terms of the resistance of disadvantaged groups. Nor have they viewed culture as an important link between a system of power relations and educational outcomes. Were they to do so, schools would be seen as contested cultural arenas, and the creation of public educational policies as political acts.

In addition, more ethnographic studies are needed, as are analyses of parent and pupil resistance to dominant group interpretations of what constitutes legitimate knowledge and culture. Institutional and structural racism in schools and school systems needs to be addressed. And the issue of differential rates of academic achievement within as well as between ethnocultural minority groups, would benefit from re-examination in the light of theories addressed above.

The areas in which research is needed and in which theories of culture, schooling and resistance could fruitfully be applied are many. Moreover, they can and should be carried out in a variety of concrete settings, in different regional contexts involving different racial, ethnocultural and linguistic groups. The task is undoubtedly daunting, but its potential outcome in terms of contributing to the understanding of schooling in a plural Canada is equally large. For, unlike, other approaches to the study of race and ethnicity in Canadian education, these theories adopt a dynamic approach, recognize the adaptive power of society, and underline the value of cultural and educational alternatives. This last point is not meant to underestimate the extent to which mainstream culture operates in the interests of dominant groups (Anglophone or Francophone). Rather it is to reaffirm the benefits for minority groups, in terms of self-affirmation and self-determination, that accrue from participation in the political process, and to underline the importance for dominant groups of incorporating different cultural options in the larger interests of achieving a just, dynamic, and ultimately viable society.

Bibliography

ANISEF, P. 1975, Consequences of ethnicity for educational plans among Grade 12 students. In A. WOLFGANG (ed.), *The Education of Immigrant Students: Issues and Consequences*. Toronto: Ontario Institute for Studies in Education.

APPLE, M. W. 1978, The new sociology of education: Analyzing cultural and economic reproduction. *Harvard Educational Review* 48(4) 495–503.

APPLE, M. W. 1979, *Ideology and Curriculum*. Boston: Routledge and Kegan Paul.

AUGUSTINE, J. 1984, Black studies or black–white studies. *Currents*.

BAGLEY, C. 1984, Education, ethnicity and racism: A European–Canadian perspective. *Currents*.

BARTON, L. & WALKER, S. (eds) 1983, *Race, Class and Education*. London: Croom Helm.

BATES, R. J. 1980, New developments in the 'new' sociology of education. *British Journal of Sociology and Education* 1(1).

BERGER, T. 1977, *Northern Frontier, Northern Homeland*. The report of the Mackenzie Valley Pipeline Inquiry: Vol. 1, Ottawa: Ministry of Supply and Services, 91–100.

BERNSTEIN, B. 1971, On the classification and framing of educational knowledge. In M. F. D. YOUNG (ed.), *Knowledge and Control. New Directions for the Sociology of Education*. London: Collier-Macmillan.

BLACK, E. R. 1975, *Divided Loyalties. Canadian Concepts of Federalism*. Montreal: McGill-Queen's University Press.

BOISSEVAIN, J. 1970, *The Italians of Montreal: Social Adjustment in a Plural Society*. Ottawa: Information Canada.

BOISVERT, D. A. 1985, *Forms of Aboriginal Self-Government*. (Aboriginal Peoples and Constitutional Reform, Background Paper No. 2). Kingston: Queen's University, Institute of Intergovernmental Relations.

BOURDIEU, P. 1966, L'ecole Conservatrice. *Revue Francaise de Sociologie* 7, 325–347.

BOURDIEU, P. & PASSERON, J. C. 1977, *Reproduction in Education, Society and Culture*. Translated from French by R. NICE, London: Sage Publications.

BOURHIS, R. Y. 1984, Social psychology and heritage language research: A retrospective view and future trends for Canada. Unpublished paper, mimeographed, prepared for the Canadian Secretary of State (Multiculturalism) following the Heritage Language Research Conference, Ottawa, May.

BOURHIS, R. Y. (ed.) 1984, *Conflict and Language Planning in Quebec*. Clevedon: Multilingual Matters.

BOWLES, S. & GINTIS, H. 1976, *Schooling in Capitalist America: Educational Reform and the Contradictions of Economic Life*. New York: Basic Books.

BRETON, R. *et al*. 1979, From a different perspective: French Canada and the issue of immigration and multiculturalism. *TESL Talk* 10, 45–56.

BROWN, C. *et al*. 1969, *Minorities, Schools and Politics*. Toronto: University of Toronto Press.

BULLIVANT, B. 1981, *The Pluralist Dilemma in Education: Six Case Studies*. Sydney: Allen and Unwin.

BURNABY, B. 1979, Roles of languages in education for native children in Ontario. Unpublished doctoral dissertation, University of Toronto.

BURNET, J. 1981, Multiculturalism ten years later. *History and Social Science Teacher*.

CANADA, BOOK I, 1967, Report of the Royal Commission on Bilingualism and Biculturalism. *The Official Languages*. Ottawa: Queen's Printer.

CANADA, BOOK III, 1969, Report of the Royal Commission on Bilingualism and Biculturalism. *The Work World*. Ottawa: Queen's Printer.

CANADA, BOOK IV, 1970, Report of the Royal Commission on Bilingualism and Biculturalism. *The Cultural Contribution of the Other Ethnic Groups*. Ottawa: Queen's Printer.

CANADA, 1982, *The Canadian Charter of Rights and Freedoms*. Ottawa: Ministry of Supply and Services.

CANADIAN EDUCATION ASSOCIATION (C.E.A.). 1984, *Recent Development in Native Education*. Toronto.

CHEECHOO, A. January, 1985, The Education Clause in the James Bay Treaty. Presentation at the Nishnawbe-Aski Nation Chiefs' Conference, Thunder Bay.

CLEMENT, W. 1975, *The Canadian Corporate Élite: An Analysis of Economic Power*. Toronto: McClelland & Stewart.

COOK, R. 1977, Presentation to First Session. *Destiny Canada Conference Final Report*. Toronto: York University. Mimeographed 19p.

COUTURE, J. E. 1979, *Secondary Education for Canadian Registered Indians, Past, Present and Future: A Commentary*. Ottawa: Department of Indian and Northern Affairs.

CUMMINS, J. 1984, *Bilingualism and Special Education: Issues in Assessment and Pedagogy*. Clevedon: Multilingual Matters.

DAHLIE, H. 1983, Confessions of an immigrant's daughter. *Canadian Ethnic Studies Journal* 15(1), 134–136.

DALE, R. *et al.* (eds) 1982, Education and the capitalist state: Contributions and contradictions. In M. W. APPLE (ed.), *Cultural and Economic Reproduction in Education*. London: Routledge and Kegan Paul.

DEHLEI, K. 1984, 'Ethnic,' 'parent,' 'community,' — the 'proper' channelling of local education politics. Unpublished paper, mimeographed, Race, Ethnicity and Education: Critical Perspectives Symposium, Toronto.

DENE NATION, 1984, Proposal for a research program to identify options and plans for Dene control of Dene education. Presented to the National Indian Education Council.

DENIS, A. B. & MURPHY, R. 1977, Schools and the conservation of the vertical mosaic. In D. J. LEE, *Emerging Ethnic Boundaries*. Ottawa: University of Ottawa Press.

DEOSORAN, R., WRIGHT, E. N. & KANE, T. 1976, *The 1975 Every Student Survey: Students' Background and its Relationship to Program Placement*. Toronto: City of Toronto Board of Education.

DURKHEIM, E. 1973, *On Morality and Society: Selected Writings*. Edited and with an introduction by R. N. BELLAH. Chicago: University of Chicago Press.

ENLOE, C. 1979, *Political Sociology of Pluralism*.

FISHMAN, J. A. 1972, *Language and Nationalism: Two Integrative Essays*. Rowley, Mass.: Newbury House.

FORCESE, D. & RICHER, S. (eds) 1975, *Issues in Canadian Sociology*. Scarborough: Prentice-Hall of Canada.

FORCESE, D. 1980, *The Canadian Class Structure*. Toronto: McGraw-Hill Ryerson.

FOUCHER, P. & THE CANADIAN LAW INFORMATION COUNCIL 1985, Constitutional language rights of official-language minorities in Canada: A study of the legislation of the provinces and territories respecting education rights of the official-language minorities and compliance with Section 23 of the Canadian Charter of Rights and Freedoms. Ottawa: Canadian Law Information Council.

GIBBON, J. M. 1938, *Canadian Mosaic: The Making of a Nation*. Toronto: McClelland and Stewart.

GIBBONS, M. 1976, Secondary education: The gathering reform. *Interchange* 6(3). Ottawa: Ontario Institute for Studies in Education, 47-54.

GIROUX, H. A. 1981, *Ideology, Culture and the Process of Schooling.* Philadelphia: Temple University Press.

GIROUX, H. A. 1983a, *Theory and Resistance in Education: A Pedagogy for the Opposition.* South Hadley: Bergin & Garvey.

GIROUX, H. A. 1983b, Theories of reproduction and resistance in the new sociology of education: A critical analysis. *Harvard Educational Review* 53(3), 257–293.

GLAZER, N. & MOYNIHAN, D. 1975, *Ethnicity: Theory and Experience.* Cambridge: Harvard University Press.

GOULD, J. & KOLB, W. L. (eds) 1964, *A Dictionary of the Social Sciences.* New York: The Free Press.

GORDON, D. 1973, *Theories of Poverty and Unemployment: Orthodox, Radical and Dual Labor Perspectives.* Lexington, Mass.: Lexington Books.

HALEBSKY, S. 1976, *Mass Society and Political Conflict: Toward a Reconstruction of Theory.* Cambridge: Harvard University Press.

HAWKES, D. C. 1985, *Aboriginal Self-government: What Does It Mean? Aboriginal Peoples and Constitutional Reform.* Kingston: Queen's University, Institute of Intergovernmental Relations.

HERBERG, E. N. 1980, *Education through the Ethnic Looking-Glass: Ethnicity and Education in Five Canadian Cities.* Unpublished doctoral dissertation, University of Toronto.

HERBERG, E. N. 1984, The vertical mosaic in flux: Ethnicity and education in urban Canada, 1959–1971. In J. R. MALLEA & J. C. YOUNG, *Culture, Diversity and Canadian Education: Issues and Innovations.* Ottawa: Carleton University Press.

HODGETTS, A. B. 1968, *What Culture? What Heritage?* Toronto: Ontario Institute for Studies in Education.

HUNT, C. L. & WALKER, L. 1974, *Ethnic Dynamics, Patterns of Intergroup Relations in Various Societies.* Homewood: The Dorsey Press.

Indian Control of Indian Education. 1972, Policy paper presented to the Minister of Indian Affairs and Northern Development by the National Indian Brotherhood. Ottawa: National Indian Brotherhood.

International Encyclopedia of the Social Sciences. 1968, *Integration.* Vol. 7. New York: The Macmillan Company, 372–386.

ISAACS, H. R. 1975, *The Idols of the Tribe: Group Identity and Political Change.* New York: Harper & Row.

ITZKOFF, S. W. 1969, *Cultural Pluralism and American Education.* Scranton: International Textbook Company.

JAENEN, C. J. 1972, Cultural diversity and education. In N. BYRNE & J. QUARTER, *Must Schools Fail?* Toronto: McClelland & Stewart.

JONES, C. & MIEDEM, W. 1984, School success and school processes with reference to minority groups in Britain and the Netherlands. Unpublished paper, mimeographed, 5th World Congress of Comparative Education, Paris, July, 1984.

KALLEN, D. B. P., KOSSE, G. B., WAGENAAR, H. C., KLOPROGGE, J. J. J. & VORBECK, M. (eds) 1982, *Social Science Research and Public Policy-Making: A Reappraisal.* Windsor, Berks: NFER-Nelson Publishing Company.

KARABEL, J. & HALSEY, A. H. 1976, The new sociology of education. *Theory and Practice* 3(4).

KARABEL, J. & HALSEY, A. H. (eds) 1977, *Power and Ideology in Education.* New York: Oxford University Press.

KING, A. J. C. & ANGI, C. E. 1968, Language and secondary school success. Report prepared for the Royal Commission on Bilingualism and Biculturalism.

KIRKCONNEL, W. 1935, *Canadian Overtones.* Winnipeg: The Columbia Press.

KORMOS, J. 1981–82, In CONNELEY *et al.* & CLAUDININ, J. (eds), *A Conceptualization of the Interface Between Teachers' Practical Knowledge and Theoretical Knowledge in Effecting Board Policy.* O.I.S.E.: Performance Report (Fourth Quarter).

LABELLE, T. J. & WHITE, P. S. 1980, Education and multiethnic integration: An intergroup relations typology. *Comparative Education Review* 24(2), 155–173.

LAMBERT, W. E. & KLINEBERG, O. 1967, *Children's Views of Foreign Peoples.* New York: Appleton-Century Crofts.

LAMONT, D., PENNER, W., BLOWERS, T., MOSYCHUK, H. & JONES, J. 1978, Evaluation of the second year of a bilingual (English–Ukrainian) program. *Canadian Modern Language Review* 34, 175–85.

LEARY, M. E. 1983, The movements are here to stay. In W. T. ANDERSON (ed.), *Rethinking Liberalism.* New York: Avon Books.

LECKIE, D. 1976, Multicultural programs in Toronto schools: A statement. *Final Report of Work Group on Multicultural Programs.* Toronto: Toronto Board of Education.

LESLIE, P. 1984, Canada as a bicommunal polity. A research report prepared for the Royal Commission on the Economic Union and Development Prospects for Canada, Kingston: Queen's University.

LIVINGSTONE, D. W. 1983, *Class, Ideologies and Educational Futures.* Sussex: The Falmer Press.

LUPUL, M. & SAVARYN, P. 1974, The politics of English–Ukrainian bilingualism in Alberta. *Ukrainian Canadian Professional and Business Federation Review.*

LUPUL, M. R. 1983, Multiculturalism and Canada's white ethnics. *Canadian Ethnic Studies* 15(1), 99–107.

LYNCH, J. & PLUNKETT, H. D. 1973, *Teacher Education and Cultural Change: England, France, West Germany.* London: Allen & Unwin.

MAGNET, J. E. 1982, Minority language educational rights. In E. P. BELOBALOS & E. GERTNER, *The New Constitution and The Charter of Rights.* Toronto: Butterworth.

MALLEA, J. R. 1977a, *Quebec's Language Policies: Background and Response.* Quebec: Les Presses de l'Université Laval.

MALLEA, J. R. 1977b, Multiculturalism within a bilingual framework: A note on the Quebecois response. *Multiculturalism* 1(2).

MALLEA, J. R. 1978, Ethnicity and Canadian education. In M. L. KOVACS (ed.) *Ethnic Canadians, Culture and Education.* Regina: Canadian Plains Research Centre.

MALLEA, J. R. & SHEA, E. C. 1979, *Multiculturalism and Education: A Select Bibliography.* Toronto: O.I.S.E. and the Ontario Ministry of Culture and Recreation.

MALLEA, J. R. 1981, Cultural diversity and Canadian education. In J. W. G. IVANY & M. E. MANLEY-CASIMIR (eds), *Federal-Provincial Relations: Education Canada.* Toronto: O.I.S.E. Press.

MALLEA, J. R. & SHEA, E. C. 1984, Intra-national comparisons in comparative education. Paper presented at the 5th World Congress of Comparative Education Societies, Paris, July 2–6.

MALLEA, J. R. 1984a, Cultural diversity in Canadian education: A review of contemporary developments. In R. SAMUDA *et al.* (eds), *Multiculturalism in Canada: Social and Educational Perspectives.* Toronto: Allyn & Bacon.

MALLEA, J. R. 1984b, Minority language education in Quebec and anglophone Canada. In R. Y. BOURHIS (ed.) *Conflict and Language Planning in Quebec.* Clevedon, England: Multilingual Matters.

MALLEA, J. R. & YOUNG, J. C. 1984, *Cultural Diversity and Canadian Education: Issues and Innovations.* Ottawa: Carleton Library Series, Carleton University Press.

MALLEA, J. R. 1986, Multicultural education: An alternative theoretical framework. In K. A. MCLEOD, (ed.) *Multicultural Education: A Partnership.* Toronto: O.I.S.E. Press.

MALLEA, J. R. 1987, Culture, schooling and resistance in a plural Canada. In J. C. YOUNG (ed.), *Breaking the Mosaic: Ethnic Identities in Canadian Schooling.* Toronto: Garamond Press.

MALLORY, J. R. 1976, The evolution of federalism in Canada. Unpublished paper presented as a part of a seminar on Federal Provincial Relations, Ottawa. Mimeographed, 15p.

MALMBERG, 1981, Letter from Deputy Minister of Education, Department of Education, New Brunswick, Dated 25th September.

MANICOM, A. October 1984, Ideology and multicultural curriculum. Race, Ethnicity and Education: Critical Perspectives Symposium, Toronto.

MANN, M. 1970, The social cohesion of liberal democracies. *American Sociological Review*, 35, 423-439.

MARJORIBANKS, K. 1970, *Ethnics and Environmental Influences on Levels and Profiles of Mental Abilities*. Unpublished doctoral thesis, University of Toronto.

MARTEL, A. 1984, 'When the sunne shineth, make hay.' Studies in Perspective and Power for Alberta Minorities and the Canadian Charter of Rights and Freedoms ' Unpublished paper, Race Ethnicity and Education: Critical Perspectives Symposium, Toronto.

MASEMANN, V. L. 1978–79, Multicultural programs in Toronto schools. *Interchange* 9(1).

McLEOD, K. A. 1979a, Schooling for diversity: Ethnic relations, cultural pluralism and education. *TESL Talk*.

McLEOD, K. A. 1979b, *Multiculturalism, Bilingualism and Canadian Institutions*. Toronto: University of Toronto, Guidance Centre, Faculty of Education.

McLEOD, K. A. (ed.) 1980, *Intercultural Education and Community Development*. Toronto: Guidance Centre, Faculty of Education, University of Toronto.

MICHAEL, D. N. 1983, Neither hierarchy nor anarchy: Notes on norms for governance in a systematic world. In W. T. ANDERSON (ed.), *Rethinking Liberalism*. New York: Avon Books.

MITTER, W. July, 1984, Multicultural education in the perspective of comparative education. *Considerations Concerning Conceptual and Thematic Foundations*. Unpublished paper, Annual Conference of the European Comparative Education Society, Wurzburg, W. Germany.

MOODLEY, K. A. 1981, Canadian ethnicity in comparative perspective. In J. DAHLIE & T. FERNANDO (eds), *Ethnicity, Power and Politics in Canada*. Toronto: Methuen.

MOODLEY, K. A. 1983, Canadian multiculturalism as ideology. *Ethnic and Racial Studies* 6(3).

MOODLEY, K. A. 1984, The ambiguities of multicultural education. *Currents*.

MORRIS, L. 1976, The politics of comparative education and language in Quebec. *Canadian and International Education* 5(2).

MURPHY, R. 1979, *Sociological Theories of Education*. Toronto: McGraw-

Hill Ryerson.

NEWMAN, W. M. 1973, *American Pluralism: A Study of Minority Groups and Social Theory*. New York: Harper & Row.

NORTHWEST TERRITORIES DEPARTMENT OF EDUCATION, EDUCATION PROGRAMS AND EVALUATION DIVISION 1978, *Philosophy of Education in the Northwest Territories*. Northwest Territories.

NOVAK, M. 1983, The new ethnicity. *New Dimensions* (Balch Institute for Ethnic Studies).

O'BRYAN, G. K., REITZ, J. G. & KUPLOWSKA, O. 1976, *Non-Official Langauges: A Study in Canadian Multiculturalism*. Ministry of Supply and Service Canada.

OGBU, J. 1978, *The Next Generation: An Ethnography of Education in an Urban Neighborhood*. New York: Academic Press.

OLSON, P. (ed.) 1981, Rethinking social reproduction. *Interchange* 12(2–3), 1–2.

OLSON, P. 1981, How working theory gets down to classrooms and kids. *Interchange* 12(2–3), 252-269.

ONTARIO SCHOOL TRUSTEES COUNCIL, 1985, Francophone association seeks more minority trustee positions. *Education Reports* 9(19).

OSSENBURG, R. J. (ed.) 1971, *Canadian Society: Pluralism, Change and Conflict*. Ontario: Prentice-Hall of Canada.

PAINCHAUD, R. 1976, The Franco-Canadians of Western Canada and multiculturalism. In *Multiculturalism as State Policy*. Ottawa: Second Canadian Consultative Committee on Multiculturalism.

PALMER, H. 1976, Reluctant hosts: Anglo-Canadian view of Multiculturalism in the 20th century. In *Multiculturalism as State Policy*. Ottawa: Canadian Consultative Committee on Multiculturalism.

PALMER, H. 1984, Reluctant hosts: Anglo-Canadian view of multiculturalism in the 20th century. In J. R. MALLEA & J. C. YOUNG (eds), *Cultural Diversity and Canadian Education: Issues and Innovations*. Ottawa: Carleton University Press.

PARSONS, T. 1959, The school class as a social system: Some of its functions in American society. *Harvard Educational Review* 29(4), 297–318.

PATEL, D. 1980, *Dealing with Interracial Conflict: Policy Alternatives*. Montreal: Institute for Research on Public Policy.

PAYNE, E. G. 1937, Education and cultural pluralism. In F. G. BROWN & J. R. LLABEY (eds), *Our Racial and National Minorities*. New York: Prentice-Hall.

PETER, K. 1981, The myth of multiculturalism and other political fables. In J. DAHLIE & T. FERNANDO (eds), *Ethnicity, Power and Politics in Canada*. Toronto, Methuen.

PIKE, R. M. 1981, Sociological research on higher education in English

Canada 1970–1980: A thematic review. *The Canadian Journal of Higher Education* 11(2), 1–22.

PORTER, J. 1965, *The Vertical Mosaic: An Analysis of Social Class and Power in Canada*. Toronto: University of Toronto Press.

PORTER, J. 1969, Bilingualism and the myth of culture. *Canadian Review of Sociology and Anthropology* 6, 111–118.

PORTER, J. 1972, Dilemmas and contradictions of multi-ethnic societies. *Proceedings and Transactions of the Royal Society of Canada*, 4th Series, No. 10.

PORTER, M., PORTER, J. & BLISHEN, B. R. 1973, *Does Money Matter? Prospects for Higher Education*. Toronto: York University, Institute for Behavioral Research.

PORTER, M. 1981, John Porter and education: Technical functionalist or conflict theorist. *Canadian Review of Sociology and Anthropology* 18(5), 627–636.

PRATT, D. 1975, The social role of school textbooks in Canada. In E. ZUREIK & R. PIKE (eds), *Socialization and Values in Canadian Society* Vol. 1. Carleton Library No. 84, Toronto: McClelland & Stewart.

Quebec Association of Protestant School Boards et al. vs Attorney-General of Quebec et al. 1984.

QUEBEC BOOK II, 1966, *Report of the Royal Commission of Inquiry in the Province of Quebec on Education*. 4 Vols. Quebec: Government of the Province of Quebec.

QUEBEC, BOOK III, 1972, *Report of the Commission of Inquiry on the Position of the French Language and Language Rights in Quebec*. Quebec: Editeur Officiel du Quebec.

REITZ, J. B. 1980, *The Survival of Ethnic Groups*. Toronto: McGraw-Hill Ryerson.

RIDEOUT, E. B. 1977, Policy changes of the ten Canadian provinces between 1967 and 1976 with respect to second-language learning and minority language education as expressed in acts, regulations, directives, memoranda and policy statements of Provincial Departments and Ministeries of Education. Department of the Secretary of State.

ROCHER, G. 1972, Les ambiguites d'un Canada bilingue et multicultural. Presented to the Canadian Sociology Association, Montreal.

SCHERMERHORN, R. A. 1970, *Comparative Ethnic Relations: A Framework For Theory and Research*. New York: Random House.

SHIBUTANI, T. & KWAN, K. M. (eds) 1965, *Ethnic Stratification: A Comparative Approach*. New York: Macmillan.

SIMON, R. I. 1983, Critical pedagogy. In T. HUSEN & N. POSTLETHWAITE (eds), *International Encyclopedia of Education*. Oxford: Pergamon Press.

SINGLETON, J. 1977, Education and ethnicity. *Comparative Education Review* 21(2/3), 329–343.

SMITH, M. G. 1965, *The Plural Society in the British West Indies*. Berkeley: University of California Press.

SMOLICZ, J. J. & SECOMBE, M. J. 1977, A study of attitudes to the introduction of ethnic languages and cultures in Australian schools. *The Australian Journal of Education* 21, 1–28.

SMOLICZ, J. J. 1979, *Culture and Education in a Plural Society*. Canberra: The Curriculum Development Centre.

SMOOHA, S. 1978, *Israeli Pluralism and Conflict*. London: Routledge and Kegan Paul.

STEIN, M. B. 1977, Bill 22 and the non-Francophone population in Quebec: A case study of minority group attitudes on language legislation. In J. R. MALLEA (ed.), *Quebec Language Policies: Background and Response*. Quebec: Centre Internationale de Recherche sur le Bilinguisme, Les Presses de l'Universite Laval.

STEPHAN, W. 1981–1983, Panem et circenses? Ten years of multicultural policy in Canada. In D. DOROTICH (ed.), *Education and Canadian Multiculturalism: Some Problems and Some Solutions*. Saskatoon: Canadian Society for the Study of Education.

STOCK, R. 1983, Multiculturalism as a community development program. Unpublished M. A. Thesis, McGill University.

SYLVESTRE, P. F. 1980, *Penetang: L'Ecole de la Resistance*. Ottawa: Editions Prise de Parole.

SYMONS, T. 1975, *To Know Ourselves*. Report of the Commission on Canadian Studies. Vols. I and II. Ottawa: Association of Universities and Colleges of Canada.

The Globe and Mail (21,02,1985) Levesque links language, constitution.

THEODORSON, G. & THEODORSON, D. (eds) 1981, *A Modern Dictionary of Sociology*. New York: Crowell.

THOMAS, B. 1984, Principles of anti-racist education. *Currents*.

TOWNSEND, R. G. 1983, Orwell and the politics of equity. *Journal of Educational Equity and Leadership* 3(3).

TRAUB, R. *et al.* (eds) 1976, *Openness in Schools: An Evaluation Study*. Toronto: Ontario Institute for Studies in Education.

TRUDEAU, P. E. 1971, *Federal Government's Response to Book IV of the Royal Commission on Bilingualism*. Ottawa: House of Commons.

TSCHANZ, L. 1980, *Native Languages and Government Policy*. London: University of Western Ontario, Centre for Research and Teaching of Canadian Native Languages.

VAN DEN BERGHE, P. 1973, Pluralism. In J. J. HONIGMANN (ed.), *Handbook of Social and Cultural Anthropology*. Chicago: Rand McNally.

WAGENAAR, H. C., KALLEN, D. B. P. & KOSSE, G. B. 1982, Social sciences
and public policy-making in the 1980s: Major findings of the SVO
workshop educational research and public policy-making. In D. B. P.
KALLEN et al. (eds) *Social Science Research and Public Policy-Making:
A Reappraisal*. Windsor, Berks: NFER-Nelson Publishing Company.

WALBERG, H. J. & MARJORIBANKS, K. 1976, Family environment and
cognitive development: Twelve analytic models. *Review of Educational Research* 46, 527–551.

WARDHAUGH, R. 1983, *Language and Nationhood: The Canadian Experience*. Vancouver: New Star Books.

WATSON, G. L. 1982, *Social Theory and Critical Understanding*.
Washington: University Press of America.

WATSON, K. 1979, Educational policies in multicultural societies. *Comparative Education Review* 15(1), 17–31.

WATTS, R. L. 1970, *Multicultural Societies and Federalism*. Studies of the
Royal Commission on Bilingualism and Biculturalism, No. 8, Ottawa:
Information Canada.

WEBER, G. 1973, *Inner City Children Can Be Taught To Read: Four
Successful Schools*. Washington, D. C.: Council for Basic Education.

WEISS, C. H. 1983, Policy research in a context of diffuse decision-making.
In D. B. P. KALLEN et al. (eds), *Social Science Research and Public
Policy-Making: A Reappraisal*. Windsor, Berks: NFER-Nelson Pub-
lishing Company.

WERNER, W. et al. 1974, *Whose Culture? Whose Heritage?* Ethnicity
Within Canadian Social Studies Curricula. Vancouver: Centre for the
Study of Curriculum and Instruction, Faculty of Education, Univ-
ersity of British Columbia.

WILLIAMS, C. H. 1980, The desire of nations: Quebecois ethnic separatism
in comparative perspective. *Cahiers de Geographic du Quebec* 24 6
(11), 47–68.

WILLIAMS, J. 1979, Perspectives on the multicultural curriculum. *The
Social Science Teacher* 8(4), 126–133.

WILLIAMS, R. 1981, *Culture*. Glasgow: Fontana.

WILLIS, P. E. 1977, *Learning to Labour: How Working Class Kids get
Working Class Jobs*. Farnborough: Saxon House.

WILLIS, P. E. 1983, Cultural reproduction and theories of reproduction.
In L. BARKER & S. WALKER (eds), *Race, Class and Education*.
London: Croom Helm.

WIRT, F. M. 1979, The stranger within my gate: Ethnic minorities and
school policy in Europe. *Comparative Education Review* 23(1), 17–40.

YOUNG, J. C. 1979, Education in a multicultural society: What sort of
education? What sort of society. *The Canadian Journal of Education*

4(3), 5–21.

YOUNG, J. C. 1983, *Multicultural Education: Dilemmas and Contradictions in an Elementary School Setting*. Unpublished doctoral dissertation. Toronto: Ontario Institute for Studies in Education.

YOUNG, J. C. 1987, *Breaking the Mosaic: Ethnic Identities in Canadian Schooling*. Toronto: Garamond Press.

Author/Title Index

Index